## Praise for *Reflections on Management*

"Watts Humphrey is best known for software engine[...]
formalize and systematize software development. But I personally have found Watts to be most inspiring when he is discussing the interpersonal, human side of the software equation. The selections in this book emphasize Watts's deep experience and deep insights into human dynamics and offer a valuable counterpoint to more programmatic writings for which he is better known."

Steve McConnell
Author of *Code Complete* and *Software Estimation*

"Watts Humphrey is doing for the software industry what W. Edwards Deming did with TQM for the automobile industry. For the software executive reading this book, it is my belief that Watts has developed a real weapon for beating your competition: a reliable, repeatable way to create software that has excellent quality *and* reduces the time to deliver it to your customer *and* lowers the cost of the entire software life cycle *and* improves employee morale. All at the same time! For the software engineer or developer reading this book, it is my belief that you are on your way to making your job more productive, satisfying, and fun."

Michael J. Cullen
Vice President, Quality, Oracle Communications Global Business Unit

"Software development is a daily collision between code, the most black-and-white of technologies, and organizations, the most idiosyncratic of human experiences. Here is the guidebook—the GPS—to success in navigating the fault line between science and art, between code and human experience. Sharing his knowledge with his characteristic style of analytics and anecdotes, Watts Humphrey imparts timeless wisdom on teams, teamwork, and creating complex software successfully and reliably."

Scott D. Cook
Founder & Chairman of the Executive Committee, Intuit Inc.

"Fledgling project managers often ask me if there is *one* book they should read; it was often difficult for me to resist the temptation to recommend Machiavelli's *The Prince*. But now I have a better, and far more positive, recommendation: Watts Humphrey's *Reflections on Management*—a collection of management gems, organized into eight broad themes, that reflect his deep insights and leadership in the field."

Ed Yourdon
Consultant and Author

"I've followed Watts Humphrey's work for as long as I can remember. I recall, in my youth, thinking that he was asking too much. Now that I'm suddenly about his age, I realize how many things he has gotten right. This collection from his most important writings should bring these ideas to the attention of a new audience: I urge them to listen better than I did."

Ron Jeffries
www.XProgramming.com

"You will enjoy this collection for its down-to-earth, accessible prose, its pragmatism, its optimism and, above all, Watts's demonstration that software quality improvement is vitally important and very achievable. Your software team can realize its full potential by applying Watts's methods. Ours did, and yours can, too."

Aidan Waine
Information Solutions General Manager, Microsoft Entertainment & Devices Division

"Software development is a team sport. Watts understands this, and better yet, he knows how to express his understanding so that others can learn from his insight. A good coach knows how to make players and other coaches more successful. Watts is one of the software profession's great coaches."

Walker Royce
Vice President, Chief Software Economist, IBM

"Watts Humphrey brings legendary experience and insight to developing great software. Whether you are in a startup or Fortune 500 company; are a developer, development manager, or CEO; use agile, lean, waterfall, or other methodology—if software and quality are important to you, you should read and pay attention to Watts's reflections."

Bill Ihrie
Software Leader/Mentor/Entrepreneur; Former SVP & CTO, Intuit

"The software engineering world owes a great debt to Watts Humphrey. His pioneering work in transforming software development practices from random and chaotic to disciplined and effective has saved billions of dollars that might otherwise have been wasted on failed projects. Bill Thomas has assembled kernels of writing by Watts drawn from his previous books and publications. The original books are all excellent, but this summation is valuable in its own right. It provides a very useful overview of Watts's thinking and the practices he has developed."

Capers Jones
Chairman and Founder, Software Productivity Research

"Watts Humphrey's contributions to professional software project management are numerous and range from CMM to Personal Software Process (PSP) and Team Software Process (TSP) practices. This book summarizes all his experiences and represents a unique body of knowledge in the area of project management. It should be the premier choice of reference for all project managers."

Prof. Dr. Dr. h.c. Dieter Rombach
Executive Director, Fraunhofer IESE, Kaiserslautern, Germany

"Watts Humphrey has been the intellectual leader and driving force behind the movement to apply process improvement to software for the last quarter century. He has a deep understanding of management based on years of personal experience, both as an executive and as an advisor to managers and executives of major corporations developing software systems. His keen insight, acquired from helping the international software community apply disciplined management processes, has been captured in his previous books and articles from which this work is derived. His advice is not limited to managers of software systems and certainly will be valuable to managers at all levels."

Larry E. Druffel, Ph.D.
Director Emeritus and Visiting Scientist, Software Engineering Institute

"Watts Humphrey shares his deep and personal understanding of what goes on in the hearts and minds of software professionals—from engineers to top managers. Watts translates this understanding into software development and management practices for producing the high-quality software products these professions innately want to produce, incorporating personal- and team-level growth, learning, and improvement. This book is certainly a collection of the best-of-the-best guidance Watts has imparted to the industry in this regard. This collection is sure to be a classic."

Laurie Williams
Associate Professor, North Carolina State University

"*Reflections on Management* is a prescription for leading people in *large-scale knowledge work*. The management themes of commitment, planning, measuring, learning, leading, and teamwork are skillfully echoed throughout the book as mutually reinforcing tiles in a mosaic serving to lock in the vision from every dimension. The book manages to accomplish this in a succinct and easily readable format."

Don O'Neill
Former President 2005-2008, Center for National Software Studies

"Watts Humphrey, who has written so much that has changed how software is managed and developed, has written another book. And once again he has written an easy-to-read, well-informed, and practical-to-use book that should help almost anyone who has worked on a software project. To say I highly recommend it is probably not saying enough. Buy it. Read it. Use it."

Ron Radice
Principal Partner, Software Technology Transition

"Watts Humphrey has made a major contribution to the understanding of software quality and how to control and improve it. Since software is the major player in contemporary computer systems, software engineers and managers will benefit significantly by following his guidelines. I particularly liked his advice that quality is a never-ending journey and his emphasis on continuous improvement of both product and process. This is important because software may last for decades. Organizations seldom discard software. They enhance and reuse it in perpetuity. Thus, software quality must be a lifecycle journey."

Norman Schneidewind
Professor Emeritus of Information Sciences, Naval Postgraduate School

"Watts Humphrey's *Reflections on Management* is a treasure trove of insights and advice from one of the leading lights in software project management. It is a must read. We are fortunate that Watts took the time to write and share his thoughts and experiences; even the chapter titles provide good advice and insights."

Victor R. Basili
Professor, University of Maryland

"Watts Humphrey's ideas, encapsulated in this book, aren't just another set of software engineering techniques and methods. Rather, they represent a way of life that encourages us to work more effectively, alone and with others; to develop our talent; and even to become better people through self-knowledge, commitment, and consideration of quality as a top priority."

Juliana Herbert
Senior Consultant, Herbert Consulting, Brazil

"Watts Humphrey's latest book has a very fortunate title; it is a genuine invitation into a transformation of how we manage our projects, our teams, and ourselves. Watts manages to draw from his rich and extensive professional experience in software development and shed light upon the road to quality. In itself, quality in software is his life quest, and Watts rightly suggests methods to accomplish this goal."

Fernando J. Jaimes
Fellow, Monterrey Institute of Technology, Mexico

"This is a wonderful book. Fans of Watts Humphrey will find new and personal examples that put the previous books in another perspective. Those who know his work but have not applied it yet may be convinced to do so now. *Reflections on Management* may be a pleasant introduction for those (if any) who do not know Watts Humphrey or his work."

Michiel van Genuchten
Manager of Digital Dentistry, Institut Straumann AG, Switzerland

"At the core, Humphrey appeals to management to create the vision of better products, greater professional fulfillment, and the joy of delivering something that is used and useful. For those of us needing a daily dose of encouragement, this book is the abundant and articulate source of it."

Stan Rifkin
Master Systems, Inc.

"*Reflections on Management* is a superbly organized book, with simple, concise chapters. It describes a comprehensive, totally disciplined approach, covering all aspects of software development, from the personal concern of the individual engineer to teams of engineers building large, significant systems. The book deserves to be on the desk of every software development manager and student."

Lawrence H. Putnam
President, Quantitative Software Management, Inc.

"How to manage technical people? How to control a software project? How to introduce and sustain disciplined software engineering practices? How to mature your organization? How to build a high performing team? How to develop excellent software? Until now you had to read five to ten books to learn all the lessons taught by the Father of Software Process. And then, of course, you had to integrate it all in your head. With this book, Watts's lifetime of lessons and advice all coalesce into one book. If you truly want to understand the discipline of software management, start here."

Dr. Bill Curtis
Senior Vice President and Chief Scientist, CAST Software
Director, Consortium for IT Software Quality

# Reflections
## on
# Management

# The SEI Series in Software Engineering

**Software Engineering Institute** | **Carnegie Mellon**

Visit **informit.com/sei** for a complete list of available products.

---

The **SEI Series in Software Engineering** represents is a collaborative undertaking of the Carnegie Mellon Software Engineering Institute (SEI) and Addison-Wesley to develop and publish books on software engineering and related topics. The common goal of the SEI and Addison-Wesley is to provide the most current information on these topics in a form that is easily usable by practitioners and students.

Books in the series describe frameworks, tools, methods, and technologies designed to help organizations, teams, and individuals improve their technical or management capabilities. Some books describe processes and practices for developing higher-quality software, acquiring programs for complex systems, or delivering services more effectively. Other books focus on software and system architecture and product-line development. Still others, from the SEI's CERT Program, describe technologies and practices needed to manage software and network security risk. These and all books in the series address critical problems in software engineering for which practical solutions are available.

PEARSON

✚Addison-Wesley  **Cisco Press**  EXAM/**CRAM**  **IBM** Press.  **QUE**  **PRENTICE HALL**  **SAMS**  |  Safari

# Reflections

---

# on

---

# Management

## How to Manage Your Software Projects, Your Teams, Your Boss, and Yourself

## Watts S. Humphrey
## with William R. Thomas

✦Addison-Wesley

Upper Saddle River, NJ • Boston• Indianapolis • San Francisco
New York • Toronto • Montreal • London • Munich • Paris • Madrid
Capetown • Sydney • Tokyo • Singapore • Mexico City

**Carnegie Mellon**
**Software Engineering Institute**

The SEI Series in Software Engineering

This publication incorporates portions of "Watts New" by Watts S. Humphrey, © 1997-2007, The Personal Software Process (PSP) (CMU/SEI-2000-TR-022) by Watts S. Humphrey, © 2000, and The Team Software Process (TSP) (CMU/SEI-2000-TR-023) by Watts S. Humphrey, © 2000, Carnegie Mellon University, with special permission from its Software Engineering Institute.

Excerpts from the following books are reproduced by permission of Pearson Education, Inc.: *A Discipline for Software Engineering; Introduction to the Personal Software Process*[SM]; *Managing Technical People: Innovation, Teamwork, and the Software Process; Introduction to the Team Software Process*[SM]; *Winning with Software: An Executive Strategy; PSP*[SM]: *A Self-Improvement Process for Software Engineers; TSP*[SM]: *Coaching Development Teams;* and *TSP*[SM]: *Leading a Development Team.*

The publisher offers excellent discounts on this book when ordered in quantity for bulk purchases or special sales, which may include electronic versions and/or custom covers and content particular to your business, training goals, marketing focus, and branding interests. For more information, please contact:

U. S. Corporate and Government Sales
(800) 382-3419
corpsales@pearsontechgroup.com

For sales outside the U.S., please contact:

International Sales
international@pearsoned.com

Visit us on the Web: informit.com/aw

*Library of Congress Cataloging-in-Publication Data*
Humphrey, Watts S., 1927-
    Reflections on management : how to manage your software projects, your teams, your boss, and yourself / Watts S. Humphrey with William R. Thomas.
        p.   cm. — (The SEI series in software engineering)
    Includes bibliographical references and index.
    ISBN 978-0-321-71153-3 (pbk. : alk. paper)
  1. Computer software—Development—Management. 2. Process control. I. Thomas, William R., 1962- II. Title.
    QA76.76.D47H863 2010
    005.1068—dc22

                                                                                    2010005103

ISBN-13: 978-0-321-71153-3
ISBN-10:      0-321-71153-X
Text printed in the United States on recycled paper at Courier in Stoughton, Massachusetts.
First printing, March 2010

*This book is dedicated to Doctors David Ryan,
Theodore Hong, and David Forcioni for the
extraordinary skill and personal consideration
they gave to my care.*

*Without them, this book would not have been possible.*

—Watts Humphrey

# Contents

# Preface

When projects go badly, our reaction is often to work harder—by which we mean work longer hours. But it's rarely that simple. Projects often go wrong at the very start, and their problems are generally symptoms of a deeply dysfunctional organization.

In a career spanning more than 60 years as a senior manager and researcher, Watts Humphrey has personally helped dozens of organizations go "from the brink of chaos to a sound, businesslike operation," as he wrote in his 2002 book *Winning with Software*. That description applied to Watts's experience with IBM, where he worked for 27 years, supervising 4,000 software professionals in 15 laboratories and 7 countries.

Later, as a senior fellow overseeing the process program at Carnegie Mellon University's Software Engineering Institute (SEI), Watts made an "outrageous commitment"—his words—to transform the world of software. Beginning in 1986, he pioneered the Capability Maturity Model (CMM), the Personal Software Process (PSP), and the Team Software Process (TSP). Those methodologies have helped thousands more organizations and engineers establish and, most importantly, commit to following effective engineering and management practices for their software projects.

Watts did not stop at describing methods for improving software engineering processes. Rather, he made it his personal responsibility to instruct "all software professionals and their managers to plan and track their work, use the best technical methods, and measure and manage the quality of this work." In addition to teaching courses and presenting at conferences, Watts invoked the power of the pen, authoring 11 books and hundreds of technical reports, journal articles, and columns.

In 2005, at a White House ceremony, Watts was awarded the United States National Medal of Technology by the President of the United States "for his vision of a discipline for software engineering, for his work toward meeting that vision, and for the resultant impact on the U.S. government, industry, and academic communities."

Much of Watts's writing focuses on detailed descriptions of the tools of process management. But an equal amount is a remarkably clear presentation of his vision for properly planned and committed work. He writes in a straightforward and personal style. He draws on anecdotes from his years at IBM and the SEI but also from his earlier experience on the Auburn University wrestling team, for example, and from his service in the U.S. military. While he often describes success, he also recounts times when he felt that he failed and how he learned to approach a problem differently the next time.

This book, drawn from Watts's books, articles, and columns, comprises a collection of advice, stories, and hard-earned wisdom, rather than specific instruction on how to implement the PSP or TSP (which are thoroughly covered in Watts's books on those specific subjects). What emerges for the reader is an understanding that successful software project management is a journey with many obstacles. To succeed, engineers must manage more than their projects. They must use their own experience and that of their teams to first understand and then plan the project ahead. They must influence their teams' attitudes and methods for doing disciplined work. And they must persuade their bosses to set aside ill-informed notions of schedules and resource commitments and look instead at hard, historical data.

The essays in Part I provide insights on types of plans and the planning process. Part II covers team building and motivation. Part III describes how to work with your managers and persuade them to use best practices. And Part IV examines your personal responsibilities, commitments, and processes.

These essays shine a light on the challenges inherent in software development and can set engineers on the road to understanding how to succeed. And while Watts's particular expertise is software, practitioners in every field of business will benefit from the wisdom and advice contained here.

*—Bill Thomas*

# Prologue

First and foremost, my thanks to Bill Thomas for all the work he did in putting this book together. He did a superb job of selecting topics and ordering the material so that it makes a cohesive whole. Even though I wrote all of the papers, reading them again brings back lots of memories of the wonderful experiences I have had in more than 60 years of professional work. In this time, I have been blessed with many opportunities and many wonderful associations. It has never ceased to amaze me how helpful people can be. Whether they are managers, peers, or subordinates, much of what I have learned has been due to the mentoring, advice, critiques, and even disagreements I have had over these years.

Second, I would like to comment briefly on where we are going. While what I have done has been exciting and rewarding, it is only a small step in the direction of the truly astounding changes coming in the not-too-distant future. Software has been hard to manage, because it is a new kind of work: large-scale knowledge work. Starting before the design of the ancient pyramids in Egypt, humans have been doing knowledge work, but on a small scale. While lots of people worked on these massive constructions, only a few of them were creative designers.

The first clues that large-scale creative work could be different were with the ancient cathedrals. While many people worked on them, the overall architecture was designed by a very few people. However, there were hundreds of skilled artisans who also did creative work. They saw themselves as creating a cathedral for God, and they worked, not for some chief engineer or boss, but for the Almighty. These workers were volunteers, and they had an overall vision and motivation that was more than just doing a job. Of course they didn't manage to tight schedules or control costs, but they did manage themselves.

What makes software more like building cathedrals than traditional work is that it is large-scale creative work. Never before have dozens, hundreds, and even thousands of people tried to work together to produce a single massive creation. Now, with the advances being made in team and multi-team management, we are learning how to do large-scale knowledge work.

Once these methods are widely practiced, we will see an enormous flowering of creative engineering. Large and complex systems will be produced on predictable schedules and for planned costs. As soon as we can do this, the possibilities of what we can design and build will be greatly expanded. We will be able to do many of the things we have thus far only dreamed about.

When we have truly mastered large-scale knowledge work, we will be ready for some unprecedented international crisis like deflecting a rogue meteoroid or reengineering the earth's atmosphere. Assuming that we have the vision and technology, we will then have the management skills to actually bring off such a massive project and to do it on a predictable schedule. Hopefully, such international crises will not arise and, hopefully, there will be no need to escape to another world or to rebuild this one, but with these new knowledge-working methods, we should be able to do it.

Finally, I have dedicated this book to three marvelously skilled doctors. About a year ago I was told I had an inoperable cancer of the liver and given three to six months to live. By a series of almost miraculous events, we found Dr. David Ryan at Mass General Hospital who introduced us to Dr. Theodore Hong, a radiologist who had invented a treatment specifically designed for my kind of cancer, and to Dr. David Forcioni, a gastroenter- ologist. Because of the care and skill of these three gentlemen, I completed the treatment and the latest reports show no sign of cancer. Dedicating this book to them is my way of saying thank you.

—*Watts Humphrey*
*January 12, 2010*

# About the Authors

**WATTS S. HUMPHREY**

Watts Humphrey joined Carnegie Mellon University's Software Engineering Institute (SEI) in 1986 after a long career as a manager and executive at IBM. Currently a Senior Fellow at the SEI, Humphrey is the founder of the SEI's Software Process Program and primary author of the SEI's software process maturity model. In 2005, he was awarded the National Medal of Technology—the highest honor given by the President of the United States to America's leading innovators. His principal focus today is on knowledge work and its impact on software and systems development.

During his 27 years with IBM, Humphrey was Director of Programming and Vice President of Technical Development. He also managed all of IBM's software product development work, including the first 19 releases of IBM's principal computer operating system, OS/360. Before his retirement, he served as Director of Programming Quality and Process. While at the SEI, he has introduced the concepts of Software Process Assessment and Software Capability Evaluation, which evolved into Capability Maturity Model Integration (CMMI). He has also led development of the Personal Software Process (PSP) and the Team Software Process (TSP).

Humphrey holds graduate degrees in physics from the Illinois Institute of Technology and in business administration from the

University of Chicago. He is a Fellow of the Association for Computing Machinery (ACM), an IEEE Life Fellow, and a past member of the Malcolm Baldrige National Quality Award Board of Examiners. Humphrey was awarded the 1993 Aerospace Software Engineering Award presented by the American Institute of Aeronautics and Astronautics and an honorary Ph.D. in software engineering by Embry-Riddle Aeronautical University in 1998. In 2000, the Boeing Corporation presented him with an award for innovation and leadership in software process improvement, and in 2010, the Illinois Institute of Technology recognized him with its professional achievement award.

Humphrey's publications include many technical papers and 12 books, including *Winning with Software: An Executive Strategy* (2001), *PSP^{SM}: A Self-Improvement Process for Software Engineers* (2005), *TSP^{SM}: Leading a Development Team* (2006), and *TSP^{SM}: Coaching Development Teams* (2006). His most recent book, *Reflections on Management: How to Manage Your Software Projects, Your Teams, Your Boss, and Yourself* (2010), is his tenth published by Addison-Wesley. He holds five U.S. patents.

## WILLIAM R. THOMAS

Bill Thomas is manager of the Technical Communications team of the Software Engineering Institute (SEI) at Carnegie Mellon University. Prior to joining the SEI in 1998, Thomas was Director of Publications for Carnegie Mellon's graduate business school for eight years. He has more than 25 years of experience in communication, public relations, and journalism, including covering business and technology for newspapers in Youngstown, Ohio, and Galveston, Texas. He holds an M.A. in communication planning from Carnegie Mellon and a B.S. in journalism from Ohio University.

# PART I
# Managing Your Projects

# 1

# Committing to High Quality

## 1.1  THE SOFTWARE QUALITY CHALLENGE

Today, many of the systems on which our lives and livelihoods depend are run by software. Whether we fly in airplanes, file taxes, or wear pacemakers, our safety and well-being depend on software. With each system enhancement, the size and complexity of these systems increase, as does the likelihood of serious problems. Defects in video games, reservations systems, or accounting programs may be inconvenient, but software defects

3

in aircraft, automobiles, air traffic control systems, nuclear power plants, and weapons systems can be dangerous.

Everyone depends on transportation networks, hospitals, medical devices, public utilities, and the international financial infrastructure. These systems are all run by increasingly complex and potentially defective software systems. Regardless of whether these large life-critical systems are newly developed or composed from modified legacy systems, to be safe or secure, they must have quality levels of very few defects per million parts.

Modern, large-scale systems typically have enormous requirements documents, large and complex designs, and millions of lines of software code. Uncorrected errors in any aspect of the design and development process generally result in defects in the operational systems. The defect levels of such operational systems are typically measured in defects per thousand lines of code. A one million line-of-code system with the typical quality level of one defect per 1,000 lines would have 1,000 undiscovered defects, while any reasonably safe system of this scale must have only a very few defects, certainly less than 10.

Before condemning programmers for doing sloppy work, it is appropriate to consider the quality levels of other types of printed media. A quick scan of most books, magazines, and newspapers will reveal at least one and generally more defects per page while even poor-quality software has much less than one defect per listing page. This means that the quality level of even poor-quality software is higher than that obtained for other kinds of human written text. Programming is an exacting business, and these professionals are doing extraordinarily high-quality work. The only problem is that based on historical trends, future systems will be much larger and more complex than today, meaning that just to maintain today's defect levels, we must do much higher quality work in the future.

To appreciate the challenge of achieving 10 or fewer defects per million lines of code, consider what the source listing for such a program would look like. The listing for a 1,000-line program would fill 40 text pages; a million-line program would take 40,000 pages. Clearly, finding all but 10 defects in 40,000 pages of material is humanly impossible. However, we now have complex life-critical systems of this scale and will have much larger ones in the relatively near future.

The eight steps required to consistently produce quality software are:

1. Establish quality policies, goals, and plans.
2. Properly train, coach, and support the developers and their teams.
3. Establish and maintain a requirements quality-management process.
4. Establish and maintain statistical control of the software engineering process.
5. Review, inspect, and evaluate all product artifacts.
6. Evaluate all defects for correction and to identify, fix, and prevent other similar problems.
7. Establish and maintain a configuration management and change control system.
8. Continually improve the development process.

While we face a major challenge in improving software quality, we also have substantial and growing quality needs. It should now be clear to just about everyone in the software business that the current testing-based quality strategy has reached a dead end. Software development groups have struggled for years to get quality improvements of 10 to 20 percent by trying different testing strategies and methods, by experimenting with improved testing tools, and by working harder.

The quality improvements required are vast, and such improvements cannot be achieved by merely bulling ahead with the test-based methods of the past. While the eight-step method presented above has not yet been fully proven for software, we now have a growing body of evidence that it will work—at least better than what we have been doing. What is more, this quality strategy uses the kinds of data-based methods that can guide long-term continuous improvement. In addition to improving quality, this strategy has also been shown to save time and money.

Finally, and most importantly, software quality is an issue that should concern everyone. Poor-quality software now costs each of us time and money. In the immediate future, it is also likely to threaten our lives and livelihoods. Every one of us, whether a developer, a manager, or a user, must insist on quality work; it is the only way we will get the kind of software we all need.

## 1.2 WHAT IS SOFTWARE QUALITY?

Software quality affects development costs, delivery schedules, and user satisfaction. Because software quality is so important, we need to first discuss what we mean by the word *quality*. The quality of a software product must be defined in terms that are meaningful to the product's users. Thus a product that provides the capabilities that are most important to its users is a quality product. Users' needs are often stated in requirements documents. Because they are so important, the development, clarification, and refinement of requirements is a major subject in itself.

It is essential to remember, however, that until you have clear requirements, you cannot develop a quality program. While you may not start with clear requirements, you must understand the requirements before you can finish.

The Personal Software Process provides the skills and practices you will need to understand the defects you inject. This will equip you to efficiently find and fix most of your defects and it will also provide the data to help prevent these defects in the future. Finally, once you can efficiently manage defects, you can devote more attention to those quality concerns that affect the usefulness and value of the programs you develop.

A software engineer's job is to deliver quality products for their planned costs and on schedule. Software products must both meet the user's functional needs and reliably and consistently do the user's job. Doing the job is a key point. While the software functions are most important to the program's users, these functions are not usable unless the software runs. To get the software to run, you must remove its defects. Thus, while there are many aspects to software quality, your first quality concern must necessarily be with its defects. This does not mean that defects are your only concern or even that they are most important, but just that you must deal with most of the defects before you can satisfy any of the program's other objectives. Even after you get the programs to work, if they have more than a very few defects, they will not work in large systems and no one will use them, regardless of their other qualities.

The reason defects are so important is that people make a lot of mistakes. In fact, even experienced programmers typically make a mistake for every seven to ten lines of code they develop. While they generally find and correct most of these defects when they compile and test their programs, often a lot of defects still remain in the finished product. Clearly, then, your first priority is to understand the defects you inject and to prevent as many of them as you can. To do this, you need to be fluent with the programming languages you use, to thoroughly understand your development support systems, and to have mastered the kinds of applications you will develop. These steps and more are required to reduce the number of defects you inject.

The term *defect* refers to something that is wrong with a program, such as a syntax error, a misspelling, a punctuation mistake, or an incorrect program statement. Defects can occur in programs, in designs, or even in the requirements, specifications, or other documentation. Defects can be redundant or extra statements, incorrect statements, or omitted program sections. A defect, in fact, is anything that detracts from the program's ability to completely and effectively meet the user's needs. A defect is thus an objective thing. It is something you can identify, describe, and count.

Simple coding mistakes can produce very destructive or hard-to-find defects. Conversely, many sophisticated design defects are often easy to find. The sophistication of the design mistake and the impact of the resulting defect are thus largely independent. Even trivial implementation errors can cause serious system problems. In fact, the source of most software defects is simple programmer oversights and mistakes. While design issues are always important, when first written, programs typically have few design defects compared to the number of simple oversights, typos, and goofs. To improve program quality, it is thus essential that engineers learn to manage all the defects they inject in their programs.

It is important to separate the question of finding or identifying defects from determining their causes. Simply counting and recording defects in software products is not specifying causes or placing blame. Defects do, however, have causes. You may have misspelled a parameter name, omitted a punctuation mark, or incorrectly called a procedure. These mistakes all cause defects. All defects, in fact, result from human errors and many of the errors that software engineers make cause program defects.

Errors are incorrect things that people do and, regardless of when or who produced them, defects are defective elements of programs. Thus, people *make* errors or mistakes while programs *have* defects. When engineers make errors that result in defects, we refer to this as injecting defects. This means that to reduce the number of defects you inject in your products, you must change what you do. To remove the defects in your products, however, often you merely have to find them. Defect removal is, therefore, a more straightforward process than defect prevention. Defect prevention is an important and a major topic that requires a comprehensive study of the entire software development process.[1]

Unless engineers find and correct the defects they inject, these defects will end up in their finished products. The problem is that it takes a lot of time and money to find and fix software defects. To produce fewer defects, you must learn from the defects you have injected, identify the mistakes that caused them, and learn how to avoid repeating the same mistakes in the future. Since defective products can be expensive to test, difficult to fix, and possibly even dangerous to use, it is important that you learn to minimize the number of defects you leave in your products.

Defects should be important to every software engineer not only because they affect the users but also because more than half a typical software organization's effort is devoted to finding and fixing defects. Because testing time is expensive and hard to predict, defects are often a major cause of cost and schedule problems.

---

1. Watts S. Humphrey. 1989. *Managing the Software Process.* Reading, MA: Addison-Wesley.

## 1.3 DEFECTS ARE NOT "BUGS"

Some people mistakenly refer to software defects as bugs. When called bugs, they seem like pesky things that should be swatted or even ignored. This trivializes a critical problem and fosters the wrong attitude. Thus, when an engineer says there are only a few bugs left in a program, the reaction is one of relief. Suppose, however, that we called them time bombs instead of bugs. Would you feel the same sense of relief if a programmer told you that he had thoroughly tested a program and there were only a few time bombs left in it? Just using a different term changes your attitude entirely.

Defects are more like time bombs than bugs. And though not all of them will have explosive impact, some of them could. When programs are widely used and are applied in ways that their designers did not anticipate, seemingly trivial mistakes can have unforeseeable consequences. As widely used software systems are enhanced to meet new needs, latent problems can be exposed and a trivial-seeming defect can truly be destructive.

At this point, those readers who have written several programs will likely shake their heads and feel I am overstating the case. In one sense, I am. The vast majority of trivial defects have trivial consequences. Unfortunately, however, some small percentage of seemingly silly mistakes can cause serious problems. In one example, a simple initialization mistake caused a buffer to overflow. This caused a railroad control system to lose data. Then, when there was a power outage, the system could not be quickly restarted and all the trains on several thousand miles of track had to stop for several hours while the needed data were reentered.

Some percentage of the defects in a program will likely have unpredictable consequences. If we knew in advance which ones these were, then we could just fix them and not worry about the rest. Unfortunately, there is no way to do this and any over-looked defect may potentially have serious consequences. Although it is true that many programs are not used in applications where failure is more than an annoyance, an increasing number are. Thus, while defects may not be an important issue for you now, they soon could be. It is important that you learn to manage defects now so you will be ready when you truly need to produce high-quality programs.

The software engineer who writes a program is best able to find and fix its defects. It is thus important that software engineers take personal responsibility for the quality of the programs they produce. Learning to write defect-free programs is, however, an enormous challenge. It is not something that anyone can do quickly or easily. It takes data, effective technique, and skill. After all, if you don't strive to produce defect-free work, you probably never will.

## 1.4 QUALITY IS A JOURNEY THAT NEVER ENDS

People tend to think of quality as a final result or destination. It is not; it is a journey that never ends. As you measure and manage quality, you will learn more about it. Then each improvement step will provide the knowledge, experience, and data needed for the next step. Focus on continuous improvement and help your team to truly believe and follow the principles of quality management. Since each person's needs are different, you must recognize where each of your developers is on this journey and help everyone take the next step. The steps in the quality journey are as follows.

1. **Test and fix.** At first, the focus of almost all software groups is on getting products to work. The developers' objective is to get the product into test as quickly as possible, and

then to test and fix (and test and fix and test and fix and . . .) until it works sufficiently well to ship to the users. At this stage, the only way that the members know to improve quality is to spend more time and money on testing. Your challenge is to move the team as quickly as possible to steps 2 through 8 of the quality journey.

2. **Inspect.** The next step is when the developers and managers start removing defects before test. This is usually done with various kinds of walkthroughs and inspections. The typical challenge in this step is to get the developers to do all of the required inspections and to do them properly.

3. **Partial measurement.** As inspection programs mature, some groups begin to measure and use inspection data both to improve the inspection process and to focus the inspections on the most defective product elements. The challenge is to get adequate data and to use these data to improve the products.

4. **Quality ownership.** As they participate in team inspections, developers may become more sensitive to the mistakes that they make and start reviewing their personal work in advance to eliminate as many of these problems as they can. Once developers reach this point, the quality of their products will quickly improve.

5. **Personal measurement.** To know how to improve the quality of their personal work, developers need objective data. The required data concern the defects they personally inject and remove, the sizes of their products, and the time they spend. The challenge is to get them to gather and use these data. As they examine the data on the defects that escaped inspections, testing, and the final user, product quality will again increase sharply.

6. **Design.** Once developers have learned to manage their coding defects, they can focus on design defects. This requires precise and well-defined design practices and sound design verification methods. The challenge is to use sound design methods for all programs—large and small—and to use sound design verification methods in all design inspections and personal design reviews.

7. **Defect prevention.** While using sound design and measurement methods will reduce defect injection rates by about two times, effective defect-prevention programs follow a structured procedure to identify process problems and make the changes needed to eliminate even more defects. The challenge is to get the defect-prevention program initiated and then to sustain and broaden it to cover the full product life cycle.

8. **User-based measurement.** Ultimately, the quality program should be driven by user-based quality measures. The principal challenge here is to understand the quality characteristics that are most important to the users and to measure these characteristics in a way that is meaningful both to you and to the users.

An Alcoa executive once invited me to visit one of their plants that manufactured sheet aluminum. He said it produced the highest quality aluminum in the world. In talking to the engineers, I was surprised to find that their quality measurements weren't about making aluminum—they concerned making cans. For example, the thicker the aluminum, the more cans cost. However, the thinner the aluminum, the more likely it was that defects in the aluminum sheet would cause an expensive and time-consuming "punch-through" that would interrupt production. Alcoa was the market leader because their quality was so good, cans made with their aluminum were thinner.

The reason that the quality journey is never ending should be clear from this example. As long as technology advances and as long as it attracts newer and different kinds of users, we will face new quality needs. The principal message from this eightfold quality journey is that it must be traveled in steps. Until the developers have made reasonable progress with step 5, they will not have the data to support steps 6, 7, or 8. So, while you should take the long view, keep your team focused on the next step in this quality journey.

## 1.5  START BY DEFINING YOUR GOAL

Goals provide an objective and a focus. They help us to set priorities and to ignore unimportant details. To achieve something important, start by defining precisely what you are trying to accomplish. Vague directions and imprecise goals waste time.

Some years ago, when I managed a software group, the marketing people came to me with an urgent need for a project. They sought a major enhancement to our recent product release and had been debating the requirements with the engineers for several weeks. They needed the product by the following November and had been unable to reach agreement. After hearing their story, I concluded that the problem was a lack of urgency. So I told the engineers and the marketers to agree on a plan in two weeks or else I would kill the project. Because both groups wanted to do the job, they skipped the normal marketing and design reviews and quickly agreed on a plan. I then funded the project, and the engineers got right to work.

As November approached, the time came to announce the product's availability. The team drafted the announcement letter and sent it to marketing for review. From this, marketing quickly realized that this product was not what they wanted. In their rush to get started, the engineers had developed what they thought was needed. It turned out, however, that they had misunderstood marketing and had built the wrong product. The entire effort was a waste of time, and the product was scrapped.

The problem here was one of goals. I had thought that the engineers and marketing people were not serious about reaching agreement and had given them an arbitrary date. Rather than take the time to truly understand each other, the two groups then quickly compromised on a vague statement that would get the project funded. Because I had made the date paramount, the focus came off the result. They finished by the date I had given them, but they built the wrong product.

Goals are important for two reasons: they provide a focus for the effort and they establish priorities. Without clear and agreed goals, engineers rarely do good work. With a clear goal, however, you know what is to be done and you have a clear direction for the work.

The goal also sets priorities. The goal is first, and everything else is secondary. Although this helps when the goal is appropriate, it is often a problem when it is not. In my case, I focused the team on a two-week objective. I assumed that they would produce a quality result, but I did not emphasize the paramount importance of producing a viable product.

Confusion about goals is a common problem in software engineering. In my early days as an engineer, managers often asked me for products on seemingly impossible schedules. One question I wish I had thought to ask was, "Does it have to work?" This would have gotten an annoyed response of, "Of course it does," but I could then have asked, "Then can it have defects, and if so, how many?" Although such questions do not make managers very happy, they at least start a discussion of the implicit goal of quality in all the work we do.

When people tell you what they want you to do, they generally have a goal but have not taken the trouble to explain it.

Even more often, they intuitively know what they want done but have not explicitly defined it. Only you can know whether you have a clear goal for what you are going to do. Even if your peers and managers think that the goal is clear, if it is not clear to you, you must speak up.

Insist on getting your questions resolved. Often, you will find that others had exactly the same questions but were afraid to ask. You can perform a real service by asking your managers to clearly define the goals that they want you to meet. If they can't do this, put together a version of what you think their goals are and check it with them before you start the work. Then make sure that you and they agree.

## SOURCES

**1.1:** From *CrossTalk*, June 2008, "The Software Quality Challenge." This article was first published in the June 2008 issue of *CrossTalk*, the Journal of Defense Software Engineering.

**1.2:** From *Introduction to the Personal Software Process*[SM], Chapter 12

**1.3:** From *Introduction to the Personal Software Process*[SM], Chapter 12

**1.4:** From *TSP*[SM]*: Leading a Development Team*, Chapter 11

**1.5:** From *Introduction to the Team Software Process*[SM], Chapter 16

# 2

# Planning for High-Quality Projects

**2.1 The Hardest Time to Make a Plan Is When You Need It Most**
When teams are under heavy pressure to commit, they must dig in their heels and insist on making a plan.

**2.2 Make Two Kinds of Plans: Period and Product**
The first is based on a period of time and concerns the way you plan to spend time during this period. The second is based on an activity, like developing a program or writing a report.

**2.3 Make Product Plans for Every Major Task**
Product plans help you to judge how much time the work will take and to track your progress.

**2.4 Review Detailed Plans with Your Management**
Few software organizations have a planning process that ensures that plans are complete, thoroughly reviewed, and properly approved, but these are what they need to manage their projects.

**2.5 Everyone Loses with Incompetent Planning**
With incompetent plans, the customers will receive late and more costly products, management will tie up excessive resources, and the developers will get a bad reputation.

**2.6 Plans Must Meet Five Basic Requirements**
A plan must be accessible, clear, specific, precise, and accurate.

**2.7 When You Can't Plan Accurately, Plan Often**
Don't let your plan be nibbled to death by small changes.

**2.8 Plans Must Be Maintained**
Even when projects are perfectly planned, changing conditions will often require plan adjustments.

## 2.1 THE HARDEST TIME TO MAKE A PLAN IS WHEN YOU NEED IT MOST

"This is an absolutely critical project and it must be completed in nine months." The division general manager was concluding his opening remarks at the kickoff for a project launch. As the Software Engineering Institute (SEI) coach, I had asked him to start the meeting by explaining why the business needed this product and how important it was to the company. As he told the development team, the company faced serious competition, and marketing could not hold the line for more than nine months. He then thanked me and the SEI for helping them launch this project and turned the meeting over to me.

After describing what the team would do during the next four days, I asked the marketing manager to speak. He described the new features needed for this product and how they compared with the current product and the leading competitor's new product. He explained that this new competitive machine had just hit the market and was attracting a lot of customer interest. He said that if this team did not develop a better product within nine months, they would lose all of their major customers. He didn't know how to hold the line.

On that happy note, we ended the meeting. The nine developers, the team leader, and I went to another room where we were to work. The team was scheduled to present its project plan to management in four days.

The developers were very upset. They had just finished one "death march" project and didn't look forward to another. After they calmed down a bit, Greg, the team leader, asked me, "Why make a plan? After all, we know the deadline is in nine months. Why waste the next four days planning when we could start to work right now?"

"Do you think you can finish in nine months?" I asked.

"Not a chance," he said.

"Well, how long will it take?"

"I don't know," he answered, "but probably about two years—like the last project."

So I asked him, "Who owns the nine-month schedule now?"

"The general manager," he said.

"OK," I said, "Now suppose you go back and tell him that nine months is way too little time. The last project took two years and this is an even bigger job. What will happen?"

"Well," Greg said, "he will insist that nine months is firm. Then I will tell him that we will do our very best."

"Right," I said, "that's what normally happens. Now who would own the nine-month schedule?"

"Oh," he answered, "I would."

"Suppose you promise a nine-month schedule and then take two or more years. Would that cause problems?"

"It sure would," Greg said. "Nobody would believe us again and our best customers would almost certainly jump ship."

"Listen," I explained, "management doesn't know how long this project will take, and neither do you. As long as you are both guessing, the manager will always win. The only way out of this bind is for you to make a plan and do your utmost to accomplish what management wants. Then, if you can't meet his deadline, you will understand why and be able to defend your schedule."

Then Ahmed, one of the development team members, jumped in. "OK, so we need a plan, but how can we make one if we don't even know the requirements?"

"Very good question," I answered, "but do you have to commit to a date?"

"Well, yes."

"So," I asked, "you know enough to commit to a date but not enough to make a plan?"

He agreed that this didn't make much sense. If they knew enough to make a commitment, they certainly ought to know enough to make a plan. "OK," he said, "but without the requirements, the plan won't be very accurate."

"So," I asked, "when could you make the most accurate plan?"

"Well, I suppose that would be after we have done most of the work, right?"

"That's right," I replied, "and that's when you least need a plan. Right now, your plan will be least accurate but now is when you most need a schedule that you can defend. To do this, you must have a detailed plan."

With that, the team agreed to make a plan.

This was one of our early Team Software Process (TSP) teams and the members had all been trained in the Personal Software Process (PSP). They then used PSP methods to make a plan that they believed was workable, and they then negotiated that plan with management. Throughout the project, they continued to use the PSP methods and, in the end, they delivered a high-quality product six weeks ahead of the 18-month schedule management had reluctantly accepted.

## 2.2 MAKE TWO KINDS OF PLANS: PERIOD AND PRODUCT

There are two kinds of planning. The first is based on a period of time, any calendar segment—a day, week, month, or year. A period plan concerns the way you plan to spend time during this period. The second kind of plan is based on an activity, like developing a program or writing a report. The products may be tangibles like programs or reports or intangibles like the knowledge you get from reading a textbook or the service you provide when working in an office.

To see the difference between period and product planning, consider the activity of reading a book. To plan this work, you would first estimate the time for the total job. For example, you might expect to take 20 hours to read the 20 chapters in an entire book. For the product plan, you would then schedule the time to do the reading, say one hour a week. The product plan for this task would then be the objective of reading the book chapters in 20 hours. The period plan would be the way you allocate reading time in one-hour weekly increments.

We all use both period and product plans in our daily lives. In business, for example, the two are related as shown in simplified form in Figure 2.1. The left half of the figure deals with the product-based tasks and the right half with the period-based tasks. These two are related as follows.

Corporate management provides funds for engineering and manufacturing to develop and produce products. Engineering develops products and releases them to manufacturing. Through the marketing group, manufacturing delivers these products to the customers, who pay for them. Engineering and manufacturing also provide product plans to finance and administration, who use the product plans to produce period plans for

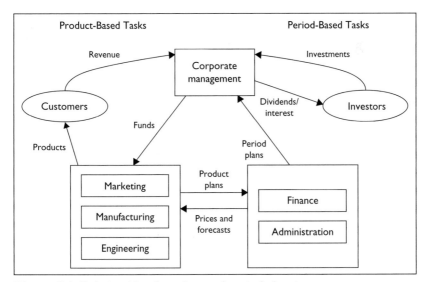

**Figure 2.1** Relationship of product and period planning

quarterly and annual revenue and expense. Finance and administration give their plans to corporate management. They also give pricing and forecast information to engineering and manufacturing so they know how many products to build each month and what to charge the customers for them.

Corporate management decides what dividends and interest to pay the investors and how much new investment they need. When they know how much money they will have in the future, corporate management can then decide on the funds to provide engineering for future product development and manufacturing, completing the cycle.

In businesses, product plans are important because they tell marketing when they can expect new products to sell to customers. They also tell finance what development and manufacturing will cost. Finance can then determine the prices they need to charge and provide accurate period plans to corporate management. Management can then allot the money engineering and manufacturing will need. If the product plans are not accurate, the period plans will also be inaccurate. Management, marketing, the investors, and even the customers will be misinformed. This in turn could mean that the necessary funds would not be available to engineering and manufacturing when they are needed. Without adequate funds, engineering and manufacturing might have to cut back their plans. When they cut back their plans, *you* could be laid off.

While this planning cycle may sound theoretical and may take several years, the threat is real. The key to job security in any business is the financial health of the organization. And a key to business financial health is accurate period and product plans. It is therefore important that engineers know how to make sound period and product plans.

While period and product plans must be related, they are different. Your work schedule, your income, and your other daily activities are governed by time periods. That is, you sleep, eat, work, and rest during certain periods of the day or week. Your expenses and income are governed by weekly, monthly, and annual schedules. You thus live in a world with period activities, rules, and constraints.

The principal purpose of your work, however, is to produce products and services of value to others. The cost, schedule, and quality of these goods or services are thus important. Since your work will be on products and your life will be in periods, both period and product plans are important to you. You cannot make a competent plan for either one without also planning the other.

## 2.3 MAKE PRODUCT PLANS FOR EVERY MAJOR TASK

Some years ago while at IBM, I was put in charge of a large software development department with many projects. Most of the projects were seriously late and senior management was very upset. My job was to straighten out the mess. The first thing I did was to review the major projects. To my surprise, none of them had any documented plans. I immediately insisted the engineers produce plans for all their projects. Never having prepared formal plans before, it took them a couple of months to do it. We even set up a special class on project planning. After they had made plans, however, they could establish realistic schedules for their work.

The act of making plans had a dramatic effect. This development group had never before delivered a product on time. Starting with their new plans, however, they did not miss a single date for the next two and a half years. And they have been planning their work ever since. Planning is a critical part of a software engineer's job, and to be an effective engineer, you need to know how to make plans. The key is practice, so to get the most practice, start making plans now and continue to do so for all your future projects.

I suggest that you develop product plans for all your projects or major tasks: writing a program, reading a textbook, or preparing a report. The product plan will help you judge how much time the work will take and when you will finish. Plans also help you track progress while doing the work.

When engineers work on development teams, they need to plan their personal work. Planning provides a sound basis for committing to completion dates, and it allows engineers to coordinate their work on joint products. Their individual product plans enable them to commit dates to each other for their interdependent tasks and to consistently meet those commitments.

Businesses use product plans for the same reasons you will: to plan and manage their work. A well-made plan includes a project cost estimate. Estimates are essential for development contracts because customers often need to know the price in advance. Estimates are also necessary when developing products. Project cost is a major part of product price and must be kept low enough for the price to be competitive in the marketplace.

Engineers also use product plans to understand project status. With reasonably detailed and accurate plans, they can judge where a project stands against the plan. They can see if they are late and need help or if they will have to delay the schedule. They may even be ahead of schedule and be able to help their teammates or deliver early. When engineers make plans, they can better organize their time and avoid last-minute crises. They are then less likely to make mistakes and will generally produce better products. Because plans are so important, you need to know how to make accurate plans. You also need to know how to compare these plans with actual results so you can learn to make better plans.

The first step in producing a product plan is to get a clear definition of the product you plan to produce. While this seems obvious, it is surprising how often people dive into the mechanics of developing a product before they define what they are trying to do. Only after you know what you want to do, should you start thinking about how to do it. That is when to start planning.

A properly produced product plan includes three things:

- The size and important features of the product to be produced,

- An estimate of the time required to do the work, and

- A projection of the schedule.

The product could be a working program, a program design, or a test plan. A product plan thus identifies the product to be produced and contains estimates of the product size, the hours to do the work, and the schedule. More complex products require more sophisticated planning and many kinds of information, such as responsibility assignments, staffing plans, product or process specifications, dependencies on other groups, or special testing or quality provisions.

## 2.4 REVIEW DETAILED PLANS WITH YOUR MANAGEMENT

Software development plans are often incomplete and inaccurate. During the 27 years when I worked at IBM, we once needed a critical new function for the OS/360 programming system. The engineering estimate was $175,000. Naively, that is all the funding I requested. Some months later, the developers found that the work would cost $525,000. They had omitted many necessary tasks from their original plan. They had forgotten documentation; testing; the integration, build, and release processes;

and quality assurance. Sure enough, however, the coding and unit test costs were about $175,000. They had made a pretty good estimate, but their plan was painfully (for me) incomplete. I had to make up the difference out of department funds.

The problem is that few software organizations have a planning process that ensures that plans are complete, thoroughly reviewed, and properly approved. Even worse, few software developers have the knowledge and experience to make sound plans. When you start a project, management typically states very clearly when they want the job done, but they are not usually very clear about much else. It is not that they are bad, lazy, or incompetent; it is just that, except for the schedule, most requirements are complex and cannot be easily described. By emphasizing the schedule, management gives the impression that it is their highest-priority concern. But, although the schedule is important, you must also address all of management's stated and implied goals. In addition, while doing this, you must do your best to meet management's desired schedule.

What management really wants is a completed project *now*, at no cost. Anything else is a compromise. However, because they know that development takes time, they will push for the most aggressive schedule that you and your team will accept as a goal. Not unreasonably, they believe that projects with the shortest schedules finish before ones with longer schedules. Therefore, they will keep pushing until they believe that the schedule is the shortest one you will agree to meet. As developers, however, we are responsible for doing the work. With an impossibly short schedule, it is difficult if not impossible to make a usable plan. Then, without a plan, we are generally in such a rush to code and test that we cut corners and don't do as good a job as we could. Such projects generally take much more time than they would with a realistic plan.

Typically, when management asks for an aggressive date, the developers tell them that this date doesn't allow enough time to do the work. Management then insists that the date is firm, and the team generally caves in and agrees to do its best. Such teams start out in trouble and almost always end up in trouble. As Greg's team found in Section 2.1, the best answer to this problem is to make a detailed plan and to review it with management. Because most managers want a schedule you *can* meet, they will negotiate a thoughtfully made plan with you. If you present a convincing case, they will then end up agreeing to your schedule. To have such a debate, however, you must know how to make a plan and how to defend it to management. PSP training provides these skills.

PSP training will help you to build the needed planning skills. Planning is the first step in the PSP for three reasons. First, without good plans you cannot effectively manage even modestly sized software projects. Second, planning is a skill that you can learn and improve with practice. Third, good planning skills will help you to do better software work. Later, on a team, the TSP shows you how to prepare for and handle the plan negotiations with management.

## 2.5 EVERYONE LOSES WITH INCOMPETENT PLANNING

In software engineering, as in other fields, our role as developers is to devise economical and timely solutions to our employer's needs. To do this, we must consider costs and schedules. The connection between cost estimating, scheduling, and the planning process can best be illustrated by an example. Suppose you want to put an addition on your home. After deciding what you want and getting several bids, most of which are around $24,000, you pick a builder who offers to do the job in three months for $20,000. Although this is a lot of money, you need the extra space and can arrange for a home-equity loan. You then sign an agreement and the builder starts the work. After about a month into the job, the builder tells you that, because of unforeseen problems, the job will take an extra month and cost an additional $4,000.

This presents you with several problems. First, you badly need the space, and another month of delay is a great inconvenience. Second, you have already arranged for the loan and don't know where you can get the extra $4,000. Third, if you get a lawyer and decide to fight the builder in court, all the work will stop for many months while the case is settled. Fourth, it would take a great deal of time and probably cost even more to switch to a new builder in the middle of the job.

After considerable thought, you decide that the real problem is that the builder did a sloppy job of planning. Although you do not know precisely what went wrong, the builder probably got low bids on some of the major subcontracts, such as the plumbing, plastering, or painting. You can endlessly debate what the job should cost, but essentially the problem was caused by poor planning. If you had originally been given the $24,000 price, you could have decided then whether to proceed with that builder and how to finance the work. The odds are good that at this point you will try to negotiate a lower price but continue with the current builder. Because the other bids were close to $24,000, you know this is a pretty fair price. You would not use this builder again, however, and would probably not recommend him to anyone else.

The problem with incompetent planning is that everybody loses: customers receive late and more costly products, management must tie up more resources, and the developer gets a bad reputation. To be successful, businesses must meet their commitments. To do our part, we must produce plans that accurately represent what we will do.

Planning is serious business. It defines commitments and supports business decisions. Well-thought-out plans will help you to make commitments that you can meet, and enable you to accurately track and report your progress. Personal planning skill will be even more important when you work on a development team. The overall team plan is most likely to be realistic when it is built from competently made team-member plans.

"The project plan defines the work and how it will be done. It provides a definition of each major task, an estimate of the time and resources required, and a framework for management review and control. The project plan is also a powerful learning vehicle. When properly documented, it is a benchmark to compare with actual performance. This comparison permits the planners to see their estimating errors and to improve their estimating accuracy."[1] Plans typically are used as the following:

- A basis for agreeing on the cost and schedule for a job
- An organizing structure for doing the work
- A framework for obtaining the required resources
- The standard against which to measure job status
- A record of what was initially committed

The connection between plans and commitments is extremely important. Every project starts as a new endeavor. At the outset, the project must be created out of thin air. New projects typically start with no staff. A manager, user, or customer must commit funds, and some workers and suppliers must be convinced to participate in the work. For substantial projects, management's

---

1. Watts S. Humphrey. 1989. *Managing the Software Process.* Reading, MA: Addison-Wesley.

first step is to assemble a planning and proposal team and produce an overall plan. Without a clear and convincing plan, they
will not be able to get funding, hire the staff, and arrange for all
the facilities, supplies, and other support needed to do the work.
Nobody wants to pay for an undefined job, and few people will
work on a project that has unclear objectives. Because an accurate plan is the essential first step in creating a successful project,
planning is an important part of every project.

## 2.6 PLANS MUST MEET FIVE BASIC REQUIREMENTS

In producing a plan, the result must meet certain requirements.
The five basic requirements for a plan are that it be accessible,
clear, specific, precise, and accurate.

### Is It Accessible?

Accessibility is best illustrated by the case of a company that was
fighting a major U.S. government lawsuit. At one point, they
were required to provide all of the historical documents that
related to a particular topic. Because the company was large, this
material was scattered among thousands of files. The cost of
searching all those files would have been prohibitive, so the
company gave the plaintiff all the files that could possibly contain any of the desired data. Even though these files undoubt-
edly contained material the company didn't want released, they
judged this problem to be minor compared to the costs of a
detailed document review. Although the plaintiff knew that
what he wanted was somewhere in the many thousands of pages
of files, he might as well not have had it. In practical terms, it
was inaccessible.

   To be accessible, a plan must provide the needed information
so that you can find it; it must be in the proper format; and it
must not be cluttered with extraneous material. Although hav-

ing complete plans is important, voluminous plans are unwieldy. You need to know what is in the plan and where it is. You should be able to quickly find the original schedule and all subsequent revisions. The defect data should be clear, and the program size data must be available for every program version. To be most convenient, these data should be in a prescribed order and in a known, consistent, and nonredundant format.

### Is It Clear?

I find it surprising that even experienced developers occasionally turn in PSP homework that is sloppy and incomplete. Some items are left blank, others are inconsistent, and a few are obviously incorrect. Sometimes, even incomprehensible notes are jotted in the margins. Such work is not data and should be rejected. If the data are not complete and unmistakably clear, they cannot be used with confidence. If they cannot be used with confidence, there is no point in gathering them at all.

### Is It Specific?

A specific plan identifies what will be done, when, by whom, and at what costs. If these items are not clear, the plan is not specific.

### Is It Precise?

Precision is a matter of relating the unit of measure to the total magnitude of the measurement. If, for example, you analyzed a project that took 14 programmer years, management would not be interested in units of minutes, hours, or probably even days. In fact, programmer weeks would probably be the finest level of detail they could usefully consider. For a PSP job that takes five hours, however, units of days or weeks would be useless. Conversely, units of seconds would be far too detailed. Here you are probably interested in time measured in minutes.

To determine an appropriate level of precision, consider the error introduced by a difference of one in the smallest unit of measure. A project that is planned to take 14 programmer years would require 168 programmer months. An uncertainty of one month would contribute an error of at most 0.6 percent. In light of normal planning errors, this is small enough to be quite acceptable. For a five-hour project, an uncertainty of one minute would contribute a maximum error of about 0.33 percent. A unit of measure of one minute would thus introduce tolerable errors, whereas units of an hour or even a tenth of an hour would probably be too gross.

### Is It Accurate?

Although the other four points are all important, accuracy is crucial. A principal concern of the planning process is producing plans with predictable accuracy. As you plan the PSP work, do not be too concerned about the errors in each small task plan as long as they appear to be random. That is, you want to have about as many overestimates as underestimates. These are called **unbiased estimates.** As you work on larger projects or participate on development teams, the small-scale errors will balance each other out and the combined total will be more accurate.

### 2.7 WHEN YOU CAN'T PLAN ACCURATELY, PLAN OFTEN

A common belief is that projects get into trouble because their requirements changed. This is an excuse. Requirements always change. Usually, the problem is with the way these changes are managed. When faced with lots of little requirements changes, it takes considerable effort to keep the plan up to date. However, if you don't, you will be working without a plan and can no longer track your work or estimate when the job will be done. While this often happens to projects, the problem is with how the project was managed—not with the requirements changes. Often, the requirements will change so often and in such small steps that you will have to constantly reassess your plan.

With a dynamic planning process, teams can assess the impact of each change and only agree to changes when management understands and agrees to the necessary schedule and resource adjustments. The team can then know the cost of each requirements change and can negotiate any needed schedule or resources requirements before committing to the change. While this sounds easy in theory, it is often exceedingly difficult in practice.

Dynamic planning will protect you from requirements creep. If you do not examine the impact of every change, you will be inundated with small changes. In effect, by accepting changes without adjusting the schedule or resources, you are telling the customer and management that changes are free. That both misleads them and invites more changes. If you do not control every change, your project will be overwhelmed with changes.

Act as if there is no such thing as a free change. This is, of course, an overreaction. There is a fine line between requirements changes and requirements clarifications. As the customer's understanding of the product matures, the only constraint on adding new functions and features is your ability to deliver. If you do not make that constraint known, you will mislead the business. The best way to do this is with dynamic planning. It is the only way to protect yourself from being nibbled to death by small changes.

The longer you work to a detailed plan, the more you will need to change it. This does not mean that you will actually change the plan, but that you will refine it. As the work progresses, the team members will better understand the work and be better able to make more detailed plans. While these small plan changes will usually be consistent with the original plan, this dynamic working plan will gradually diverge from the plan you made during the launch.

Suppose that, after a few weeks of work, one team member completes her planned tasks and is ready to start on some new ones. If the rest of the team is still following its prior plan, it might not make sense to conduct a team relaunch. Rather than have this one developer work without a plan, she could add some near-term tasks to her current plan and continue working. To allow for this possibility, it is generally a good idea to extend the team's planning well beyond the planned relaunch date. Rather than plan all of the future work in detail, however, the later tasks could be kept in larger chunks and only refined when needed. In fact, developers often find it desirable to defer detailed planning for their larger tasks until shortly before they start to work on them.

While it is often possible to keep extending the current plan, it is not a good idea to defer the team relaunch for too long. The relaunch is needed not just to update the plan, but to update the team's goals and to review the team's risks and role assignments. It is also a good time to assess the work that has been done and to agree on how to do better work during the next project cycle.

### 2.8 PLANS MUST BE MAINTAINED

Although planning is essential for well-run projects, detailed plans are generally accurate for only brief periods of time. As developers work, they learn more about the job and its many parts, and they see how long it takes to do various kinds of tasks. They also learn more about the product and have a better idea of how to develop it. Another factor affecting plans is that the developers' organizations and projects will change and evolve. Thus, even when projects are perfectly planned, changing conditions will often require plan adjustments. So, unless the members regularly adjust their plans, these plans will become less and less relevant to their work.

Even without external changes, the team's detailed plans will become inaccurate. Some developers will finish tasks ahead of their plans, and others will fall behind. There will also be estimating errors and overlooked tasks. The more detailed the plans and the longer they are used, the more inaccurate they will become. This is a problem because the team members' work must be synchronized. They must come together for design reviews, inspections, and management reviews. They must also coordinate to produce the team's products and to meet project milestones. As the workload becomes unbalanced, the schedule for these synchronization points will then be determined by the developers who are furthest behind. Periodic replanning is the easiest and quickest way to address this imbalance problem.

Managers get nervous when developers update their plans. They intuitively expect that every replan will extend the schedule. However, once teams learn to make accurate plans and to work to these plans, they can replan without significantly changing their committed schedules. If the original plan was competently made, if it was based on historical size and task-hour data, and if there were no significant external changes, the baseline plan should be pretty accurate. Then, the team's plan changes will only involve the normal estimating fluctuations at the detailed level plus any resource and requirements variations.

At the detailed level, team plans must change on a regular basis. If the plans are based on average historical data, about half of the developers should finish their tasks early and the other half late. However, on average the team's overall plan will still be consistent with the baseline plan. The problem is that some developers will occasionally have several consecutive tasks that take longer than planned. They will then fall behind schedule and, unless their team reassigns some of their tasks, these normal workload fluctuations could lead to serious workload imbalances. Teams should regularly identify the members who are early and can handle additional workload and those who are behind and need tasks offloaded. If teams do not keep their detailed plans in balance, some members will eventually fall so far behind that they will delay the project.

## SOURCES

**2.1:** From *PSP<sup>SM</sup>: A Self-Improvement Process for Software Engineers,* Chapter 1

**2.2:** From *Introduction to the Personal Software Process<sup>SM</sup>*, Chapter 4

**2.3:** From *Introduction to the Personal Software Process<sup>SM</sup>*, Chapter 5

**2.4:** From *PSP<sup>SM</sup>: A Self-Improvement Process for Software Engineers,* Chapter 4

**2.5:** From *PSP<sup>SM</sup>: A Self-Improvement Process for Software Engineers,* Chapter 4

**2.6:** From *PSP<sup>SM</sup>: A Self-Improvement Process for Software Engineers,* Chapter 7

**2.7:** From *TSP<sup>SM</sup>: Leading a Development Team,* Chapter 8

**2.8:** From *TSP<sup>SM</sup>: Coaching Development Teams,* Chapter 18

and have not established a pecking order or agreed on how to work together as a cooperative team. The group's energies are concentrated on internal issues. They are not yet ready to get to work.

When teams do not get right to work, it usually means that one or more members are uncomfortable or unclear about their roles or assignments. Get these issues on the table and deal with them directly. With small teams, such problems can usually be handled quite quickly. On larger teams, however, it usually takes a great deal longer. This is both because there are more people involved and because there are often several subteams with separate team leaders. If any subteam leader has a role or responsibility concern, those issues must be resolved before their teams can become work groups. Once the team leaders are in agreement, their subteams can start to resolve their internal issues.

Process issues concern responsibilities and roles. The best way to deal with these issues is to have a team assign specific role responsibilities to its members and to develop detailed plans. When all team members have assigned role responsibilities and when the team has made a detailed plan for doing the work, the process issues will generally go away. This approach will handle most, but not all, process issues.

### The Combat Group

The combat group is fighting an external threat. This threat is typically perceived as an attack on the team's mission or responsibilities. The team may think that its very existence is at stake. Mack's team was working as a subcontractor on part of a large project. His group was in a separate department from the larger group, and all the developers in this department worked for him. Mack's people were just finishing one job and there was no other immediate next job for them to do.

The project manager wanted Mack's entire staff transferred to his department. However, Mack's management wanted to keep them as a separate development group. Mack was in a difficult political position. While he was committed to doing the subcontract, he knew that his management wanted his group to remain separate from the larger central development group.

Mack was a developer and didn't like politics. He started sending an alternate to the weekly project management meetings and began to deal very formally with the rest of the project. When Mack's team made a major change in its development strategy, Mack decided not to make a new plan. This made status hard to measure and progress almost impossible to track. The program manager became concerned about Mack's dependability and raised the issue with senior management. When rumor of this escalation leaked out, Mack's team felt even more threatened.

Combat groups are often difficult to deal with. They feel threatened and often behave illogically. This generally makes the situation worse, and may actually increase the threat. As the threat increases, the team members submerge their internal process issues and concentrate on defending the team. It is then almost impossible to find out what bothers the developers. They are concentrated on repelling the perceived attack and will view any outsider as part of the threat. Even the coach will have trouble helping teams that are in combat mode.

The best way to deal with a combat group is to identify the perceived threat and to deal with it directly. Either get management to make the feared change or demonstrate that the team's fears are unfounded. The unknown is generally more frightening than the known, so by confirming a team's fears you will actually reduce the threat. This converts an unknown and potentially frightening risk into a known and specific issue to be addressed. By confirming the team's fears and working with the team on a plan to handle those fears, you can show that the situation is not as bad as the team had feared.

When a team is behaving like a process or a combat group, it will not work effectively. Its energies will be largely devoted to addressing the perceived internal or external threat. While the team may seem busy and focused, the members will be uneasy. They will know that the team is not performing effectively. Examine the group's behavior and talk to the members, both individually and as a group. Try to understand what troubles them and then, together with the team leader, directly address their concerns.

## 3.11 TEAMS ADOPT VARIOUS WORKING STYLES

Even when they are working effectively together, teams can adopt various working styles. There is no right or wrong style, and each team style is appropriate under different conditions. By understanding these styles, you can guide your teams to adopt the working styles that best handle the situations they currently face. Larry Constantine defines the four styles of team behavior as the *open group*, the *random group*, the *closed group*, and the *synchronous group*.[19]

These four styles are the extremes. Real team styles generally occur in combination, as shown in Figure 3.1, and it is rare to have a team behave purely in a closed style with no synchronous, open, or random characteristics. Typically, teams will operate in some position nearer to the middle of this figure.

---

19. Larry L. Constantine. 1993. "Work Organization: Paradigms for Project Management and Organization." *Communications of the ACM* 36, no. 10, 35–43.

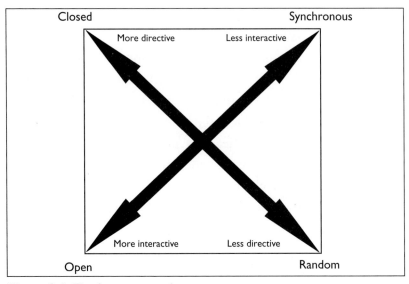

**Figure 3.1** The four group styles

### The Open Group

In the **open group**, the members are all capable of doing the various team tasks. They flexibly adjust their behavior to support or assist each other as needed. When Mary's team was in the early stages of product planning, it was a good example of an open group. The developers were estimating the size of the product they were going to produce. The design manager first outlined the conceptual design and then briefly described each component's function. He then asked who had worked on something similar and could provide data to help them make a size estimate.

The developers all participated in the discussions, and although their individual estimates varied widely, the team quickly arrived at a consensus estimate for every component. The entire estimate was completed in less than an hour, and the total size was estimated at about 100,000 lines of software code. When the project was completed over a year later, the team found that their original estimate was within 20 percent of the final product's size.

Although the conclusions reached by open groups are often sound, when one or a few team members have special knowledge, they can bias the results. One team, for example, followed a similar size-estimating procedure, but Craig had much more experience than the others. He dominated the estimating discussion and his views were generally accepted by the group. Since Craig had written a great many programs and had already worked on the exploratory design and proposal for this project, his views were given considerable weight. However, it turned out that Craig was not a very good estimator. He generally opted for the lowest estimate, and this estimate ended up being less than half the final size of the product.

When one member dominates the team in any activity, the team will start operating as a closed group. If a different style would be more appropriate for addressing the current task, help the team and team leader move the team to a more appropriate style. If this doesn't work, consider breaking the group into two or three subgroups and have each of them address the topic independently. Then have the entire group reconvene to combine the subgroups' results.

### The Random Group

The **random group** style is a brainstorming style for finding a creative solution to a difficult or controversial problem. When meetings are well run, with a precise schedule and agenda, people are often reluctant to disrupt the proceedings. More chaotic meetings are much less intimidating. Since random group meetings are purposefully chaotic, it is easier for people to speak up.

While random groups often involve considerable contention, there is usually a free flow of ideas. The objective is to take full advantage of everyone's knowledge and experience. There is also often a requirement that the group reach consensus on the final result. When random groups are given the time to fully explore a topic, they generally reach consensus on a conclusion, and their conclusions are normally sound.

An example of a random group is Sally's team. While the team was discussing project risks, Sally stood at the front of the group and asked the members to randomly suggest risks, which she listed on the board. She let the team members discuss whatever risks they thought of, but she prevented them from evaluating or comparing any items. She asked that they hold any discussion for later so that they could initially focus on ideas. She kept the team in brainstorming mode until everyone had run out of ideas. When all of the risks they could think of were listed on the board, Sally led the group in an open-group evaluation of each item. At this point, the group efficiently eliminated duplicate items and ranked the remaining risks for likelihood and impact. By consciously switching the team's working styles, Sally quickly led the team through the risk assessment process and ended up with team consensus on the result.

### The Closed Group

The **closed group** is essentially managed from the top down. It has a specific job to do and a clearly defined way to do it. There is little need for discussion or creativity, and the challenge is to get the job done as quickly and efficiently as possible. Sally's team is also an example of a closed group. After it had completed TSP launch planning and was preparing the presentation to management, Sally needed help in producing the materials. As team leader, she had decided to make the entire presentation but had little time to prepare. She outlined the presentation, listed the tasks to be done, and assigned each task to a team member. If any member did not know how to handle that task, she gave it to someone who did. There was no debate, the tasks were clear, and the assignments were made quickly and efficiently.

Groups often fall into the closed style when there is a crisis or some specific task that needs to be done in a hurry. Closed groups can be very efficient for relatively brief and well-understood tasks, but this style should be limited to short-term and fully defined activities. Otherwise, teams can degenerate and cease behaving as creative and thinking teams. They then lose their commitment to delivering quality products and stop behaving like self-directed teams.

### The Synchronous Group

The **synchronous group** consists of relatively independent individuals who each have a job to do. They have the skills and resources to do their own tasks, and they have little need to interact with the other team members. They each operate essentially alone, only calling for help when they need it. An example of this type of group is Sally's team during the production of the management presentation materials. The developers each had specific assignments, and they carried them out independently. While all of the pieces had to fit together into the final presentation, that was Sally's concern, and there was no need for the developers to interact with each other. This allowed them to produce the required materials in the limited time available.

## 3.12 PROPERTIES OF SELF-DIRECTED TEAMS

While it seems desirable to have a motivated and energetic team, why is it important to you? The best way to describe the value of such a team is with an example.

My very first development team was building a complex crypto-graphic system for the U.S. Army Signal Corps (see also Section 4.1). We had just started life-testing the first model when a hurricane hit. This was some time ago and weather forecasting was pretty crude, so the storm was a complete surprise. By Saturday morning, I got so worried that I went to our basement laboratory in an old building in downtown Boston to see how the equipment was doing. Even though no one had called them, the entire team was there.

We spent the next several hours turning off and disconnecting the equipment and getting everything up on benches, desks, and crates. Water had been seeping up through cracks in the floor, and by the time we were done it was ankle deep. It took a lot of work for all of us, but everything was saved and the project finished on time.

This is characteristic behavior of self-directed teams: the members sense what is needed without being told, pitch in to help, and do whatever is needed to get the job done. This is their job, they own it, and they intend to finish it. This is why self-directed teams will stick together right to the end of the job. Typically, employee turnover on self-directed teams is zero. The members may know that the team will be dispersed, the organization disbanded, or the contract transferred, but this is their project and they intend to see it through.

While a self-directed team would be useful for any kind of job, such teams are essential for complex and creative development work. This kind of work requires everyone's wholehearted participation. If team members are not committed to the job and in agreement with its goals, they will not strive to do a superior job. Quality work is not done by mistake. It is done by thinking, caring, and motivated people. Self-directed teams have some special properties that set them apart from all other teams. The following are the five properties of self-directed teams.

1. A sense of membership and belonging

2. Commitment to a common team goal

3. Ownership of the process and plan

4. The skill to make a plan and the discipline to follow it

5. A dedication to excellence

Such teams typically devise their own development strategies, develop their own plans, and are motivated to do superior work.

The members of a self-directed team are part of a cohesive and distinct group, and there is no question about who is on the team and who is not. All of the members share a common bond of membership and they seem to have a special communication medium. They are so familiar with the job and with each other that they can almost speak in shorthand. The most impressive aspect of a self-directed team is the way that its members work together. Cooperation is the essence of teamwork and it is the key to building the required trust and spirit. Self-directed teams are close-knit and cohesive groups and, while the members may not all be close friends, they are all valued contributors.

Cohesion is the bond among members that knits them together. Cohesion requires contact and close association. The team members must share a common workspace, see each other often, and communicate freely and openly. You can't legislate cohesion; it is a consequence of the team's working context. Cohesion is a fundamental property of a self-directed team.

Team cohesion is strengthened by the support the members provide to each other. Human beings are social animals and few people like to work entirely by themselves, at least not for very long. Team membership provides a comfortable human environment and a source of mutual commitment, support, and motivation. All of the members of such teams make a special effort to meet their obligations to their teammates.

When a team does not have clear boundaries and its members seem to randomly drift on and off the team, no one can assume responsibility and the members cannot rely on each other. This is the principal problem with part-time team members. When developers are simultaneously assigned to several projects, they have split loyalties and their teammates cannot rely on them for support and assistance. They are rarely available when needed and no one really knows whether they are on the team or not.

While it is normal for developers to have some demands from prior projects, these must be the exception and every team member should have a principal project assignment. Teams with a substantial number of part-time members can rarely jell. The reason is that it is hard for someone to feel committed to a project when management is unwilling to make it their principal job.

Self-directed teams share a common commitment to a goal. While the goal has importance to the organization, its principal value to you is to provide the focus for the team. The team members' motivation results from the common commitment they have made. Once they have decided to accomplish this goal, they will do their utmost to bring it off.

To maintain this commitment, the team must receive feedback on its work. Whoever heard of a winning team that didn't know the score? To be motivated, teams must know when they are ahead and when they are behind. They also must see progress every day. Only then can teams continue pushing to achieve their goals. For high personal and team performance, feedback is the single most important ingredient (see also Section 3.6).

Goal tracking and feedback are critically important. Effective teams are aware of their performance and can see the progress they are making toward their goals. In a study of air defense crews, those with frequent and precise feedback on goal performance improved on almost every criterion. This compares with the stable, unimproving performance of crews that did not get feedback.[20]

Another property of self-directed teams is ownership. This is not just any job these teams are doing; it is *their* job. They feel responsible for it and have decided just how to do it. Such teams speak of their work with a special pride. To have this sense of ownership, all of the team members must participate in defining their own processes, producing their own plans, and tracking and reporting on their own work. The members must be solely responsible for doing this job and they must know that nobody else will do it. This responsibility provides a sense of personal importance and a feeling of self-respect.

Finally, when a team has a defined process and a detailed plan, the members will know what to do. While this seems obvious, it is fundamental. When a group is unsure about what to do and it doesn't know where to get guidance or help, it cannot jell. It is merely a group of confused people looking for direction. Under these conditions, the members will work to different priorities, not support each other, and often work counterproductively. Following a process and a plan will provide stability and build the team's motivation and energy. To be self-directed, teams need a common goal, they must have a defined and understood process, and they must also have a detailed plan.

Self-directed teams are especially well suited for creative development work. They define the process and the plan for doing the work and they have the discipline to follow that process and plan. Discipline, in fact, is what separates the experts from the amateurs in any professional field. Their willingness to

20. Watts S. Humphrey. 2000. *Introduction to the Team Software Process*[SM]. Boston, MA: Addison-Wesley.

rehearse, to practice, and to continually improve is what makes them experts. Studies have shown that the principal distinction between world class performers and those who finish in the middle of the pack is their disciplined behavior.[21]

The final property of self-directed teams is their dedication to excellence. For teams to work cooperatively and to maintain their energy and motivation, all members must strive to do more than their share of the work. Everyone volunteers for the tough assignments, pitches in, and contributes to the best of his or her ability. The spirit and energy of such teams depend, however, on the quality of everyone's work. If a member does sloppy work, makes frequent mistakes, and causes excessive rework, it wastes everyone's time. If this happens often, everyone will know the source of the problem and will resent it. Poor work by any team member can quickly destroy the team's spirit. Then you will no longer have a self-directed team.

While these five properties—membership, commitment, ownership, discipline, and a dedication to excellence—are essential, they are not enough. Self-directed teams, above all, must have effective leadership. The team leader must motivate, coach, drive, and urge the members to perform to the best of their abilities. In short, the quality of your team's work depends, more than anything else, on your leadership. If the team is properly trained and built and if you are an effective team leader, it will perform superbly, almost regardless of the challenges it faces. But if you do not provide effective leadership, your team will not excel and it may not even do a competent job.

While providing such leadership may seem like a daunting challenge, particularly if you have never been a team leader, leadership is not that difficult. At least it is not difficult if you

---

21. Atul Gawande. 2002. "The Learning Curve." *The New Yorker.* January 26, 52–61.

know how to go about it. While all of the conditions described in this chapter are needed for self-directed teams, meeting these conditions is not as difficult as it may seem. Teams like to jell, and when they are given the proper leadership and support, they generally will.

## SOURCES

**3.1:** From *TSP$^{SM}$: Coaching Development Teams*, Chapter 1

**3.2:** From *Managing Technical People: Innovation, Teamwork, and the Software Process*, Chapter 14

**3.3:** From *Introduction to the Team Software Process$^{SM}$*, Chapter 2

**3.4:** From *TSP$^{SM}$: Coaching Development Teams*, Chapter 2

**3.5:** From *Introduction to the Team Software Process$^{SM}$*, Chapter 17

**3.6:** From *Introduction to the Team Software Process$^{SM}$*, Chapter 2

**3.7:** From *Introduction to the Team Software Process$^{SM}$*, Chapter 2

**3.8:** From *Introduction to the Team Software Process$^{SM}$*, Chapter 17

**3.9:** From *TSP$^{SM}$: Coaching Development Teams*, Chapter 2

**3.10:** From *TSP$^{SM}$: Coaching Development Teams*, Chapter 2

**3.11:** From *TSP$^{SM}$: Coaching Development Teams*, Chapter 2

**3.12:** From *TSP$^{SM}$: Leading a Development Team*, Chapter 3

# 4

# Being an Effective Team Member

**4.1 Good Team Members Do Whatever Is Needed**
This example shows teamwork at its finest.

**4.2 Commitment Is an Ethic That Must Be Learned**
Responsible commitments must be based on a plan to do the work.

**4.3 A Goal Is Something You Want to Achieve**
Goals clearly define the end that we desire and establish a priority for the required work.

**4.4 Every New Idea Starts as a Minority of One**
You have a responsibility to share your ideas with the team.

**4.5 All Team Members Should Contribute What They Know**
Aircraft flight crews illustrate the importance of real participation.

**4.6 Team-Building Requires Active Involvement of All Team Members**
The principal objective of team-building is to get all the team members to actively participate in the team's work.

**4.7 Good Negotiators Have an Effective Strategy**
This example shows how principled negotiation avoids polarizing positions.

**4.8 One Non-Participant Will Reduce Everyone's Performance**
Every member has an obligation to help maintain order, so you need to distinguish between disruptive behavior and real concerns.

**4.9 Ask for Help and Offer Yours**
It is surprising how often software engineers struggle alone to solve a difficult problem.

## 4.1 GOOD TEAM MEMBERS DO WHATEVER IS NEEDED

One of the finest examples of teamwork I know of was displayed on my very first development project (see also Section 3.12). The contract was for a large digital communications system that was planned for U.S. Army field use by the Signal Corps. The eight engineers on the team were mostly raw recruits, but the two technicians were old hands. Once, when we burned out the last precision resistor, they saved the day. The Signal Corps was coming for a review in one week, and the early demonstration model wouldn't work without these parts. When Purchasing said they couldn't get new resistors in time, the technicians found some in only half an hour. We never asked where they came from, but we learned to trust their "midnight requisition" system.

This team did whatever was needed without question or direction. Just after we finished the first system and put it under test in the basement laboratory, a hurricane struck, and floods were predicted for the weekend. Even though no one was called, everyone showed up on Saturday morning. By late afternoon, water was actually squirting up through cracks in the cement floor, and all power had to be shut off. Everyone splashed around in that cold, dark basement, moving heavy equipment onto improvised stands; but none of it was damaged.

At the end of the project, volunteers were needed to help with the environmental tests. The equipment had to operate from minus 10 degrees Fahrenheit to plus 132 degrees Fahrenheit. while the humidity was maintained at a constant 90 percent. This wasn't too bad during the heat-up cycle, but on the way down, it actually snowed in the chamber! Since someone had to be in there with the equipment all the time, this promised to be a tough assignment. Everyone wanted to go, however, but the medical department allowed only four of the team into the chamber. The equipment came through the tests with flying colors and so did the people.

## 4.2 COMMITMENT IS AN ETHIC THAT MUST BE LEARNED

When one person makes a pact with another and both of them expect it to be kept, that is a commitment. The following is a good example.[1]

In one case, a programming project was threatened by a change in an engineering schedule. The programmers were completing the control program for a special-purpose machine when the engineering manager called to say the first test machine would be delayed by two months. Since they were about to start testing, the programmers were in a panic. The programming manager had been an engineer, however, and he knew what to do. He called the engineering manager and told him the programming schedule was totally dependent on delivery of the test machine, and if it didn't arrive on time, he would call an immediate meeting with the president to tell him the cause of the delay.

In the turmoil that followed, the engineers found they could keep the date for the test machine after all. They had needed an additional machine for the service department and thought they could divert the programming machine to solve the problem. When forced to take responsibility for the delay, they found another answer. Engineering had committed the current schedule to the president and they were proud of always meeting their commitments.

As a team member, you should make responsible commitments and strive to meet them. This is the only way that teams can operate. The members must trust one another to do what they say. Responsibly plan to finish your committed work on the allotted date. Some organizations have a tradition of never missing

---

1. Watts S. Humphrey. 1997. *Managing Technical People: Innovation, Teamwork, and the Software Process.* Reading, MA: Addison-Wesley, 14.

commitments. When someone has a problem, everyone offers to help. Commitment is an ethic that must be learned. After you see its benefits, however, you will never want to work any other way.

Responsible commitments must be based on a plan to do the work. You make a plan based on what you know of the job and your experience with similar work. Then you examine your other work and compare it to the priority of this job. Only then can you responsibly say when you will complete the job. This is what it takes to make a responsible commitment.

The motivation to meet a commitment is largely the result of the way it was made. First, the commitment must be freely assumed; that is, in making a commitment, you must have had a choice. Second, the commitment is public. You have personally made the commitment, and your credibility is on the line.

Third, to make a responsible commitment you must prepare; that is, you define and estimate the work and conclude you can do it. If several people are involved, all of them must participate in this planning and their views must be carefully considered. It takes time to make everyone familiar with the job and what they are expected to do, but this is the only way to establish a solid commitment foundation.

After you and your instructor or manager or customer or teammates have agreed on the commitment, the final step is performance. When everything goes according to plan, there is no problem; but this is rarely the case. There are always surprises, and in technology there is an unwritten law that all surprises involve more work. With experience, engineers learn to allow for this, but their plans can never be entirely accurate. A final crash effort is thus often needed to meet the agreed-on deadline. With good planning, however, the plans are usually close enough so that the job can be finished with a modest final push.

When the smoke has cleared, the team should reassess the work to understand what went wrong and how to make a better commitment next time. The estimates should be reviewed to see what was overlooked, and the contingencies should be revised to include the new experiences. By comparing actual performance with the estimates, engineers soon learn to make better estimates. This is why the people who will do the work should make their own plans: to learn how to consistently make commitments they can meet.

## 4.3 A GOAL IS SOMETHING YOU WANT TO ACHIEVE

The dictionary defines a goal as "the result or achievement toward which effort is directed."[2] Goals concern results and efforts, but most importantly they concern direction. Goals provide direction and focus for our efforts. They clearly define the end that we desire and establish a priority for the required work.

Goals also imply several other things. For example, you need to know whether you have achieved the desired result and where you are along the way. Are you winning or losing and are your efforts likely to be successful? All of these—the result, direction, measurement, and effort—are involved in setting and achieving goals.

Goals are useful for individuals. Few would argue that, without a goal, it is impossible to strive. Without some objective, all the effort seems pointless and a waste of time. After all, if the effort doesn't get you anywhere, why bother? Thus, a goal concerns a destination, and this destination must be some place or some state that you really would like to achieve. This could be losing weight, getting a higher score, or delivering a product, but the goal provides a concrete objective toward which to strive.

---

2. *Random House Dictionary of the English Language*. 1983. New York: Random House.

Another way to think about goals is in the negative. A key reason given when the presumed better competitor loses in boxing, track, or any other sports competition is that he or she did not want to win badly enough. Similarly, in building products, it is widely accepted that when people don't strive to build quality products, they generally won't. In fact, they really cannot. Challenging goals are not achieved by mistake. If you don't consciously strive for them, you almost certainly will not achieve them.

So, goals are not just an invention of management, they actually satisfy a fundamental human need. The goal defines our purpose: why we are here, why we are working, or what we intend to achieve. Simply put, without a goal, you cannot succeed and, if you cannot succeed, why try? Goals are the motivators for human endeavor. They energize our lives and our work. They give us purpose. Achieving a goal provides a sense of achievement and satisfaction. Goals are important to people and they are even more important for teams.

Teams need goals for all of the same reasons that individuals do. In addition, goals provide a common working framework for the team. The goal is something that everyone agrees on and can cooperatively work to achieve. The goal helps to resolve issues. Does this activity move the team toward the goal or would something else be more effective? If some action does not help to achieve the goal, why bother doing it? After achieving a goal, the team members have something to celebrate. It was hard work, but they brought it off. It was a team achievement and everyone shares in the celebration and in the credit.

Without a common goal on which all members agree, you have a loose collection of individuals who share only a common trait or facility; you cannot have a team. It would be hard to imagine an athletic team where the members did not all share a common goal, agree on precisely what that goal was, and know exactly what the score was at every point in the play. In addition, precise and timely feedback on goal status is an essential prerequisite for high-performance teams.

## 4.4 EVERY NEW IDEA STARTS AS A MINORITY OF ONE

After communication and commitment, the third teamwork obligation is participation in the team's activities. Teams provide more than just bodies; they also offer a range of skills and perspectives. Because of its combined knowledge and experience, a team can be a powerful resource, but only if properly used. For example, when the team members meet to solve a problem, produce a design, or make a plan, it is important for everyone to contribute ideas. Although there is no special trick to doing this, the primary need is for the meeting leader or facilitator to ensure that everyone participates. If someone tries to say something and is drowned out, the facilitator should note the fact and call on this member as soon as there is an opportunity to do so.

In team problem solving, some members may be so accommodating that they do not defend their own views. If you have a strong opinion and are not convinced that the team has considered it, do not cave in too quickly. Try to understand the facts and ask the team to help you understand why you should change your mind.

Keep the discussion on a rational plane and search for a logical reason. Remember that every new idea starts as a minority of one. If you are the one, you have a responsibility to that idea and to the team. Often, if you merely stop and ask the team members to explain their logic, entirely new options show up. The team may take a different and totally unanticipated direction. This is called *synergy*. One idea spawns questions. In answering them, you raise further questions. Each question stimulates more thought, and these thoughts produce better answers. As a team member, part of your job is to stimulate this discovery process.

I know of no statistics on this subject, but in many juries everyone initially agrees with one position except for a single holdout. In a surprising number of cases, however, when the final verdict is rendered, that one holdout has swung the entire jury to unanimous agreement with the reverse position. Although such holdouts can be powerful, they need support. You may not agree with the holdout's position, but you should make sure that it is explored. You could be the critical ally that this individual needs to persist. Although your support may not swing the decision, it is important that the team fully consider and understand all the team members' viewpoints.

## 4.5 ALL TEAM MEMBERS SHOULD CONTRIBUTE WHAT THEY KNOW

The experiences of aircraft flight crews illustrate the importance of real participation. Valente tells the following story:

> Tapes show that the co-pilot on an Air Florida jet that crashed in a snowstorm in Washington, D.C., in 1982 raised questions about the amount of slush on the wings before takeoff. Again during takeoff, he repeatedly warned that something was "not right." Through it all the captain remained silent until the co-pilot called out, "We're going down!" "I know it," were the captain's last words.[3]

The most common type of airliner accident is called "controlled flight into terrain"—in other words, a properly functioning aircraft is flown into the ground. Almost always, the cause is a flight crew teamwork problem. Often, a study of the black box

---

3. Judith Valente and Bridget O'Brian. 1989. "Airline Cockpits are No Place to Solo." *The Wall Street Journal.* August 2: B1.

tapes shows that at least one member of the flight crew knew about the problem but failed to take action in time.

To have a smoothly functioning team, it is crucial for every team member to contribute what he or she knows. If no one is paying attention, do whatever it takes to get attention. Under these conditions, think of yourself as the co-pilot. Make sure you are heard and understood. Don't give up. Get the team's attention.

The stories of airline flight crews have two messages. The first is one we have already discussed: speaking up and getting the team's attention. The second message is about paying attention and accepting help. One of the major problems with airline flight crews is the common attitude of "I don't need help; I can do it myself." This hotshot image of being fully competent and self-sufficient is common to fighter pilots who are used to flying alone. The fighter-pilot ideal is known as having the "right stuff." Unfortunately, this Lone Ranger image is also common in many other professions, including programming. Another story by Valente illustrates the advantages of accepting help:

> As soon as he heard the aircraft's tail engine explode, Capt. Dennis Fitch, a United DC-10 training pilot aboard as a passenger, sent word to the cockpit that he was available to help. Capt. Alfred C. Haynes, a 33-year United veteran, readily accepted. The airliner, with the hydraulics that allow pilots to control it crippled, was spiraling downward at about 2,400 feet a minute.

> Scrunching down on his knees between the crew seats, Capt. Fitch experimented with the throttles. The two pilots found that they could keep the nose of the plane up if they advanced the two remaining engines to full throttle, and that they could steer with great difficulty, by varying the thrust of each engine.

The manufacturer had relayed word to the crew that a DC-10 without hydraulics could not be flown. But, with the help of a third pilot, this crew was able to bring the plane in to a successful crash landing. Of the 296 people on board, 185 survived, including the three pilots.

The point is that being self-sufficient is important in some situations, but trying to be self-sufficient during a crisis can be dangerous. When you are in trouble, ask for and accept help. When someone is offering to help, pay attention. The odds are that you need it even if you don't think you do.

## 4.6  TEAM-BUILDING REQUIRES ACTIVE INVOLVEMENT OF ALL TEAM MEMBERS

Just as teamwork requires the participation and active involvement of all team members, so does team-building. In fact, the principal objective of team-building is to get all the team members to actively participate in the team's work. The team-building obligations are as follows.

- Accepting responsibility for a team role and performing that role to the best of your ability
- Participating in establishing team goals and plans and striving to meet these goals and to follow the plans
- Building and maintaining an effective and cooperative team

### Accepting and Performing a Team Role

All team members should have defined roles, though most teams do not have such definitions. But even informal team roles must fit the team's mission, mesh with the other roles, and match members' personal talents and abilities. Your role could be vague or open-ended, such as figuring out what tests to run or controlling the design standards. Because roles are important to the proper functioning of a team, the TSP defines them.

There are several reasons for assigning roles to all team members. First, most projects include much more than development work. Plans must be developed and tracked, data gathered and stored, changes managed, standards defined, support facilities obtained, and so on. If no one is responsible for these tasks, they will either not get done or they will be handled in a haphazard way. This situation is generally inefficient and frequently results in important tasks being overlooked or done at the wrong time.

The second reason for defining roles is so that the team members will feel responsible for their own working environment. If there are problems, the engineer with the relevant role will quickly understand the problem and fix it. When the team is responsible for its own support, it is more likely to do the job properly.

Third, no one can design, implement, or test full time. When they try to do so, engineers get stale and are more likely to make mistakes. The various tasks required to perform the role responsibilities provide a ready source of tasks that engineers can interweave with their development work. This approach not only accomplishes the important role tasks, but it also provides a useful break from development work. Surprisingly, you will find that by occasionally taking such a break, you will actually get more done and you will make fewer mistakes.

### Establishing and Striving to Meet Team Goals

An effective team can do more together than the members could do by themselves. The goal is superior performance. If you merely wanted more arms and legs, that would be a working group and not a team. Katzenbach has studied many teams, and he notes that any team can be successful as long as it is focused on performance.[4] The key, he says, is to have specific, measurable

---

4. Jon R. Katzenbach. 1992. "The Right Kind of Teamwork." *The Wall Street Journal.* November 9: A10.

goals. They cannot be just any goals, however; they must be specific. With a clear charter and tough, specific performance goals, teams can work miracles. The key is to make sure that everyone understands and agrees to the goals.

An aggressive goal can be motivating, but it can't be just any goal. It must be something that the team agrees is important, and it must be something the members feel they can accomplish. It is here that planning comes in. While making a plan, the team members are devising a way to meet the goal. Until they have estimated how much work it will take and have decided who will do each part, the goal is only a hope. When they have a plan, however, they have the knowledge and understanding to commit themselves to meeting the goal.

### Building and Maintaining the Team

The third team-building obligation is to build and maintain the team. If your team has not coalesced into a coherent and cooperative group and you think you know why, do something about it. One way to do this is to meet as a team and to ask some questions.

1. Do we have clearly defined goals?

2. Are the goals important to all the team members?

3. Have we made a plan to achieve these goals?

4. Was everyone involved in making that plan?

5. Do we all agree that this is a good plan?

6. Have all team members committed to do their best to meet the plan?

7. Is everyone making an effort to meet the plan?

8. Are all team members following the commitment guidelines outlined earlier, either meeting their commitments or warning in advance of problems and negotiating a new date?

9. Do we all meet at least once a week to review status, plans, and issues?

If the answer to any of these questions is no, that should give you a good idea about the source of the problem. If you can answer yes to all the questions, your team will likely jell, given enough time.

## 4.7 GOOD NEGOTIATORS HAVE AN EFFECTIVE STRATEGY

It is not just a matter of luck that some people are better at negotiating than others. Either through experience or training, good negotiators have learned to use an effective negotiating strategy.[5] Take the example of Tina, the team leader, who was helping the engineers on an industrial team select their roles. Most of the roles were quickly settled, but two engineers wanted the design manager role. Al was an older engineer with a great deal of design background, and Jeanne was a newer engineer with high potential but not much experience. Although Al would most likely be the best design manager, Tina did not want to hurt Jeanne's feelings.

Tina's approach to this negotiation followed the guidelines for principled negotiation, shown in Table 4.1. First, she avoided positions. Although both Al and Jeanne started by stating opposing positions, Tina did not even discuss these positions. She immediately got them talking about interests. She did this by asking them to explain why they wanted the job.

Al said he had a lot of background with this kind of product and had a number of design ideas. In fact, he had even built a prototype of some of the key functions. Jeanne, however, said

---

5. Roger Fisher and William Ury. 1981. *Getting to Yes: Negotiating Agreement Without Giving In*. Boston: Houghton Mifflin, 13.

**Table 4.1** Negotiation strategies

| Element | Soft Negotiation | Hard Negotiation | Principled Negotiation |
|---|---|---|---|
| Participants | Participants are friends | Participants are adversaries | Participants are problem solvers |
| Goal | Agreement | Victory | A wise outcome reached efficiently and amicably |
| Approach | Make concessions to cultivate personal relationships | Demand concessions as a condition of the relationship | Separate the people from the problem |
| Trust | Trust others | Distrust others | Proceed independent of trust |
| Focus | Change your position easily | Dig in to your position | Focus on interests, not positions |
| | Make offers | Make threats | Explore interests |
| Bottom Line | Disclose your bottom line | Mislead as to your bottom line | Avoid having a bottom line |
| Options | Accept one-sided losses to reach agreement | Demand one-sided gains as the price of agreement | Invent options for mutual gain |
| Deciding | Search for the single answer: the one *they* will accept | Search for the single answer: the one *you* will accept | Develop multiple options to choose from; decide later |
| Criteria | Insist on agreement | Insist on your position | Insist on objective criteria |
| Will | Try to avoid a contest of will | Try to win a contest of will | Try to reach a result based on standards independent of will |
| Pressure | Yield to pressure | Apply pressure | Reason and be open to reasons; yield to principle, not pressure |

she had a lot of knowledge about design methods but was principally interested in learning more about design. She felt that being design manager would give her more design experience.

Then Tina asked the team members for alternative ideas for solving the problem. They made several suggestions. The idea that seemed most attractive was to have Al be the design manager with Jeanne as his alternate. That would allow Jeanne to lead the design work when Al was not there and would involve Jeanne in all the design meetings and discussions.

Next, Tina discussed the criteria for a solution. She was careful to keep personalities out of the debate and to focus on the criteria for the best result. Everyone, including Al and Jeanne, agreed that the choice should be based entirely on the likelihood of getting the highest quality design.

In exploring the options against the criteria, Jeanne wasn't sure how the proposed option would work. She and Al talked about how they would work together, and they both finally agreed on a reasonable approach. At that point, Jeanne agreed that Al was probably a better choice and that she would be willing to be the alternate design manager.

The reason that principled negotiation is effective is that it avoids the polarization of positions. When the two sides to a negotiation work from opposing positions, they have no way to agree. A win for one is a loss for the other. The only way out of this dilemma is to move from positions to interests. What is each party after, and what do they really want? Note that to find out what they really want, the team must practice empathic or active listening (see also Section 3.8).

The basis for principled negotiation is a recognition that a position is only one way to satisfy an interest. By focusing on interests instead of positions, you free up the debate while obtaining the information needed to arrive at a sound and effective solution.

Although these debates can sometimes take a great deal of time, the key is to stay objective and to take as long as is required to arrive at a solution that all parties will accept. When the team realizes that the team leader will keep the meeting in session until the question is settled, even if it takes until late at night, people start to get much more reasonable. Then issues can be settled quickly.

This exhaustion strategy can work well, but only if the leader can stick to the principled negotiation strategy. As long as the team can objectively debate the issues and look for creative solutions, the members will continue to work on the problem. If positions get frozen, however, the meeting will quickly degenerate and people are likely to get angry and storm out. Principled negotiation may take a lot of time, but it is much more effective in the long run.

## 4.8 ONE NON-PARTICIPANT WILL REDUCE EVERYONE'S PERFORMANCE

Sometimes, teams don't jell because one or two members refuse to participate or to carry their fair share of the workload. Team members can often be more effective than managers or team leaders in resolving such problems. In fact, disruptive or uncooperative behavior is often intended to impress the rest of the team. Therefore, the team itself may be the only group that can address the problem. Because every member has an obligation to help maintain order, you need to distinguish between disruptive behavior and real concerns. If someone has an unexplored issue and is being squelched, provide support. If the person is being disruptive, think of ways to support the team leader.

This is the principal area where academic teams differ from working teams. On an industrial team, the members are paid to do a job. If someone doesn't perform, he or she could soon be out of a job. When a team member does not show up, consistently fails to meet commitments, or is otherwise uncooperative, the team should be very direct. Explain the problem and define what the member needs to do to improve. Offer to help if that seems appropriate, but make it clear that if there is no immediate improvement, the team will take the problem to management.

This approach is almost always effective. In most cases, with the team's help, you can get initially uncooperative members to perform. When you cannot, go directly to management and explain the problem. Be specific about the problems and suggest an improvement program if you can. Then management will generally talk to the engineer and explain that without improvement, he or she will likely be dismissed. This is almost always effective in changing the team member's behavior.

In team courses, the situation is entirely different. Here, the team members pay for their education and the faculty provides the courses. Although poor performers can be given lower grades, they cannot be fired. As a result, peer pressure is much less likely to be effective for changing the behavior of difficult team members.

The reason is that some people have been doing the minimum that they can get by with all their lives. They have probably learned to ignore badgering by their parents and teachers and are unlikely to change now just from peer pressure. Usually, the only thing that works in these cases is a serious threat, such as being dismissed from a job. Clearly, this will not work with students.

In addressing such problems, student teams should again start by reviewing the problem with the nonperformer and offering to help if needed. Start by discussing the problems and asking whether the student is having trouble. The student might have had a heavy workload that week, been sick, or had a family crisis.

If the problem is truly temporary, one such discussion is usually all that is required. If the problem is not temporary, make it clear that adequate performance is required. If the student does not respond quickly, go to the instructor and ask that the student be removed from the team. Don't worry about being short-handed. Experience shows that just one drone on a team will reduce everyone else's performance. In fact, removing the non-performing member will usually improve overall team performance.

## 4.9 ASK FOR HELP AND OFFER YOURS

An important responsibility of team members is to call for help. It is surprising how often software engineers struggle alone to solve a difficult problem. Generally, these are problems that others have faced and know how to solve. Had they asked for help in time, they could have quickly solved the problem. By the time others learn about the problem, however, it is often too late to recover.

As a team member, remember that *you are not alone.* If you insist on playing the Lone Ranger, sooner or later you will get into a fix that you cannot get out of by yourself. By waiting to ask for help, you may have destroyed the team's ability to meet its goal.

For software, the support that the team gives to its members is critical. In addition to your official team role, you must be a team citizen and give some of your time to helping everyone else. This means that you should participate in inspections, give advice, and contribute to design sessions. Almost everyone can occasionally use advice or assistance, and peer reviews are an essential part of a mature process. When you have the support of your team, you are far more likely to perform at your best.

The essence of support is to help people to be what they can become. One of my earliest memories is of failing first grade. My dad told me that I had not failed; rather, the school had. He moved the family to a different town, where my brothers and I attended a school that gave me special help. I did not find out until much later that I had a learning disability. Although learning to read was one of the most difficult things I ever did, the most important lesson in my life was that my dad believed in me. That allowed me to believe in myself, and from then on I was able to learn.

This is the key to providing effective support: helping your teammates to believe in their own abilities. When they believe in themselves, they are more likely to strive to do superior work. They may doubt their ability to handle some tasks, and they may need help and guidance, but the key thing to remember is that people can do much more than they think they can.

When engineers know that you and your teammates believe in them, they will often perform beyond what you or they thought possible. Goethe once said, "Treat a man as he is and he will remain as he is. Treat a man as he can and should be and he will become as he can and should be."[6]

## SOURCES

**4.1:** From *Managing Technical People: Innovation, Teamwork, and the Software Process*, Chapter 14

**4.2:** From *Introduction to the Team Software Process*[SM], Chapter 17

**4.3:** From *TSP*[SM]: *Coaching Development Teams*, Chapter 7

**4.4:** From *Introduction to the Team Software Process*[SM], Chapter 17

---

6. Stephen R. Covey. 1989. *The 7 Habits of Highly Effective People: Powerful Lessons in Personal Change*. New York: Simon & Schuster, 301.

**4.5:** From *Introduction to the Team Software Process<sup>SM</sup>*, Chapter 17

**4.6:** From *Introduction to the Team Software Process<sup>SM</sup>*, Chapter 17

**4.7:** From *Introduction to the Team Software Process<sup>SM</sup>*, Chapter 17

**4.8:** From *Introduction to the Team Software Process<sup>SM</sup>*, Chapter 17

**4.9:** From *Introduction to the Team Software Process<sup>SM</sup>*, Chapter 17

# 5

# Leading and Coaching Your Teams

## 5.1 Leadership Makes the Greatest Difference
When development projects fail, it is almost always because of poor leadership.

## 5.2 The Three Principal Motivators Are Fear, Greed, and Commitment
Team commitments seem to have a much greater motivating power than individual commitments.

## 5.3 Making and Sustaining Commitments
Commitments must be voluntary, visible, credible, and owned by the people who do the work.

## 5.4 Create a Sense of Urgency with Short-Term Goals
Weekly status tracking and periodic management reviews can help your team meet its intermediate dates.

## 5.5 Involve the Entire Team When Selecting New Team Members
Team members may know more about the candidates than you do, so listen carefully.

## 5.6 The Power of Coaching
My college wrestling coach inspired the team because he really cared about how each of us did.

## 5.7 Techniques for Getting All Team Members Involved
Newcomers are often unsure of their roles, so they are reluctant to speak up or to voice opinions. Encourage them to speak up.

## 5.8 Put Teams to Work During the Storming Phase
Don't rush teams through this phase, but help them understand and address their frustrations. Then get them focusing on how to solve their problems rather than merely complaining about them.

## 5.1 LEADERSHIP MAKES THE GREATEST DIFFERENCE

In the fifty-plus years since I started doing development work, I have worked on, led, managed, directed, assessed, or coached literally hundreds of creative development teams. While I have drawn many lessons and guidelines from this experience, the one clearest message is that leadership makes the greatest difference. Without exception, truly creative work is done by teams with very capable leaders. What is most interesting, however, is that these great leaders are generally ordinary developers like you and me, but when thrust into a leadership position, they do an outstanding job.

What is equally interesting is the converse. When development projects fail, it is almost always because of poor leadership. I have seen many smart and dedicated developers make basic leadership mistakes. This is a shame, because it is totally unnecessary. Leadership is not a complex subject and anyone can be a great leader.

When I was first made team leader, I had just joined a development group at my first job and did not know any of the team members or have the vaguest idea what they were doing or why. I didn't even understand the organization or the technology. While things worked out well in the end, it was due more to the marvelous people on my team than to any special insight or skill on my part.

However, I have found that this is not unusual. Given half a chance, your people will be very helpful, even when you are the new boss and they know much more about the job than you do. While there will be occasional exceptions, people want to like and respect you and they want you to succeed. They will tolerate your dumb questions and silly mistakes as long as you are willing to admit your mistakes and laugh at your goofs. Be honest about what you know and don't know, and assume that management had a good reason to make you the team leader.

After I had worked for a few years, I was asked to lead a larger group in another department. I knew the people pretty well and also knew a great deal about the job. This time, however, my reception was not nearly as smooth. One of the more experienced members of the new group was older than I, and he and several team members thought that he should have been the team leader instead. While this situation took a bit longer to straighten out, the team finally came to terms with my new role and we established a good and productive working relationship.

The way teams perform depends to a great extent on how they relate to their leadership. However, I have found that the way your team relates to you will depend on a host of factors, many of which you can influence but some you cannot.

## 5.2 THE THREE PRINCIPAL MOTIVATORS ARE FEAR, GREED, AND COMMITMENT

An interesting aspect of motivating developers and other creative people concerns technical challenge. New and inexperienced developers are often reluctant to take on unfamiliar challenges. They lack the self-confidence and job security required to take the risk. More experienced developers, however, are often excited by new technical challenges and are eager to learn new methods and techniques. On the other hand, the same experienced developers will likely feel that repeated assignments of similar work are not interesting or motivating.

Some tasks are motivating because of working conditions. Developers will gladly join one team while a similar assignment on another team will offer little or no attraction. Motivation is a complex mix of talents, experiences, preferences, and attitudes, and what will motivate one developer at one time may not be motivating to the same developer at a different time or under different conditions.

For the workplace, the three principal motivators are fear, greed, and commitment. Fear can be an effective motivator, and a team leader who is also a manager can resort to it when needed. All you have to do is to say, or even just imply, that the team members could lose their jobs if they do not finish a task as directed.

While this is rarely a productive tactic, it is guaranteed to get a reaction. However, the reaction is often not what you would want. The reason is that fear engenders unthinking reactions rather than thoughtful creative actions. When management resorts to threats and fear, they force their people down the Maslow hierarchy. Now, instead of self-actualization and respect, they are concerned with membership and even personal safety. This can often induce protective or even irrational behavior.

A good example is the manager who launched a new quality initiative. He decided to measure the quality of each developer's work by the number of defects found in team inspections of his or her programs. He announced that each developer's job evaluation would be partly based on this quality measure. Thereafter, except for an occasional requirements mistake that could be blamed on somebody else, nobody reported any defects for any of their teammates. Since inspections were no longer useful for finding defects, they became an expensive waste of time. However, because the inspections were no longer finding defects, the quality of the team's products got worse instead of better. Fear is not a useful motivator, at least not for technical work.

Greed, or at least the normal desire for more money, is the most common workplace motivator. It is, after all, the basis for salary increases, sales commissions, and annual bonuses. People do tend to perform in ways that they hope will get them more money. However, these greed-related motivation systems have one big disadvantage: the reward must be coupled to the desired performance. This requires a measurement and evaluation system that permits management to calculate the appropriate reward for any given level of performance.

The problem with reward-based motivation systems is that few human activities are straightforward enough for simple evaluation measures.[1] Even piecework systems that base the pay on the number of products produced usually motivate counterproductive behavior. For example, in a typical manufacturing plant with a piecework pay system, people often produce exactly the standard quota every day; no more and no less. Anyone who produces more, in a desire for more money or promotion, could be castigated by the rest of the group. The workers know, or at least they suspect, that if anyone demonstrates an ability to produce more than the norm, quotas would soon be increased and they would have to produce more product to earn their current pay. The workers' fear of group displeasure overrides the motivation to get more money.

A motivation system that uses financial or similar rewards switches the employee's objective from the accomplishment to the reward. This substitutes greed for self-actualization. Under

---

1. Robert D. Austin. 1996. *Measuring and Managing Performance in Organizations.* New York: Dorset House Publishing.

these conditions, people will try to maximize their expected rewards while minimizing the effort required. While this may sound like what you want, it really isn't. For example, if you rewarded the developers for the volume of code they produced, you could expect to get at least some programs that had a lot more lines of code than would be needed by clean designs.

Since greed and fear are not appropriate motivators for development work, this leaves us with the third motivator: commitment. A **commitment** is a promise to do something. What makes commitments motivating is the person's or team's desire to do what was promised. As we shall see, the level of motivation is almost entirely a function of how the commitment was made. The elements of commitment are negotiation, agreement, and performance.

### Negotiation

Two parties are generally involved in a commitment negotiation. One party, the buyer, describes what is desired and tries to convince the other, the supplier, that the commitment is important and worthwhile but not that hard to meet. The supplier then responds with a proposal. If the proposal does not completely satisfy the buyer, the parties negotiate until they either agree or break off negotiations.

### Agreement

The essential ingredient for an agreement is credibility. To reach agreement, the supplier must somehow convince the buyer that he or she can be trusted to perform as promised, and the buyer must assure the supplier that he or she can and will pay the agreed price. Since consistently demonstrated performance leads to credibility, credibility is related to performance. The buyer's ability to pay is usually easy to confirm, but if the buyer is not already confident of the supplier's ability, the parties must find some way to satisfy the buyer's need for a credible commitment. Typical ways to demonstrate this are with detailed plans, guarantees, or penalty clauses.

## Performance

After the buyer and supplier come to agreement, the next step is doing the agreed work. This is where motivation comes in. The supplier, or in our case the development team, has made a promise to the buyer, or management, and is expected to do whatever is required to meet that commitment. For development work, this is critical. On development projects, for example, there are usually surprises, and there is an unwritten rule of engineering that all surprises cost time and effort. So, regardless of how carefully the commitment was made, a final Herculean effort is often needed to meet the committed date. But why do the developers make a crash effort to finish? The reason is that they are motivated by their commitment.

## Team Commitments

People react in different ways to commitments. Some make extraordinary efforts to do absolutely everything they say they will do; others seem to forget commitments the minute they make them. After you have been let down a couple of times by someone, you learn not to trust that person's commitments. So the person making the commitment is key: is this someone you can trust? What is most interesting about commitments, however, is that team commitments seem to have a much greater motivating power than individual commitments.

Within broad limits, the bigger the team and the stronger its commitment and cohesion, the greater the motivating force. It seems that when all the members have participated in making a team commitment, and when the entire team depends—at least to some extent—on every member to meet that commitment, the entire team is highly motivated to do so.

## 5.3 MAKING AND SUSTAINING COMMITMENTS

The four parts of making credible team commitments are shown in Figure 5.1.

The first requirement for motivating development teams is that the commitment be voluntary. This suggests that managers ask for commitments rather than dictate them. Also, of course, these managers must not direct, force, or otherwise browbeat their people into agreeing to a commitment. In short, voluntary means voluntary.

Second, the commitment must be visible. This means that development teams must be somehow involved in negotiating their own commitments and that the negotiation process must be transparent and have documented results.

Third, the commitment must be credible. While there are many ways to make commitments credible, one of the most reliable ways is to support it with a detailed plan. By producing a

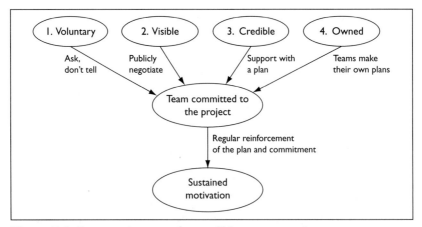

**Figure 5.1** Four requirements for credible team commitments.

plan, you and your team demonstrate that you have thought through what must be done and are convinced you can do it with the resources and on the schedule to which you have committed.

Fourth and last, the commitment must be owned by the people who will do the required work. The only way to reliably meet this condition is to have the people who will do the work develop the plan to meet the commitment. These people must also be involved in negotiating the commitment with management.

These four conditions provide the basis for *making* a team commitment, but they do not provide all of the conditions necessary to *sustain* this commitment throughout a long and challenging project. For that, you need some way to periodically reinforce the commitment throughout the job. This reinforcement must be frequent enough so the team members can see the immediate next steps required to meet the commitment.

To provide timely feedback, break the overall commitment into milestones that can serve as intermediate progress measures. Then identify and plan the steps to meet each milestone commitment. Next, manage the work according to the plan and track progress weekly or even daily. Finally, all of the team members must believe that the commitment is achievable. If at any time the team begins to doubt the feasibility of completing the job as planned, address that concern directly. If the team members start to feel discouraged and defeatist, their work will suffer.

## 5.4 CREATE A SENSE OF URGENCY WITH SHORT-TERM GOALS

Schedules slip a day at a time.[2] Few projects can detect a one-day schedule slip. To have any chance of meeting the project's schedule, you must meet all of its intermediate schedules. Because

---

2. Frederick P. Brooks, Jr. 1995. *The Mythical Man-Month: Essays On Software Engineering, Anniversary Edition*. Reading, MA: Addison-Wesley.

projects have many interrelated tasks, and because it is rarely clear how each of these tasks contributes to the overall project, developers rarely appreciate the importance of completing each day's scheduled tasks on that day. At least they won't understand it until the project is near completion.

Another leadership challenge is helping the team members set intermediate goals. While there is no general way to do this, one strategy is to break large projects into multiple releases and to establish planned dates for each release. Then hold periodic management review meetings on team performance against these goals. Before each review meeting, discuss intermediate goal status with the team and agree on recovery plans for any that are late. If the reviews are reasonably frequent and if the checkpoints are not too far apart, you can generally motivate the team to complete each intermediate goal before the next review.

People generally react to crises and little else. A slip of a few days on a one-year project will not generally cause much concern. However, a slip of a few days on a checkpoint that is due next week can be much more motivating. It will be even more motivating if there is a management review of the team's status next week, and if everyone who is late will have to produce and defend his or her recovery plan.

Even if there is no near-term build or release, you can create a sense of urgency. However, to be motivating, the urgent needs must be real, credible, and publicly committed. If, for example, your team establishes a date to release the initial design specification and you commit this date to management, you can track status against this commitment in each weekly team meeting. If you then schedule a management review, you can probably maintain the team's focus on this design specification commitment.

Suppose, however, that the design specification involved several months of work. What could you do? One approach would be to work with the team to establish checkpoints for each of the specification's chapters. Examples could be the first overall draft, the team inspection, and the final release. You could follow a similar strategy with almost any checkpoint.

While this strategy will expose you to missing an occasional checkpoint, weekly status tracking and periodic management reviews can help your team meet its intermediate dates. This will help you and the team maintain the urgency and motivation needed to complete the project on schedule.

## 5.5 INVOLVE THE ENTIRE TEAM WHEN SELECTING NEW TEAM MEMBERS

While there is no foolproof way to identify suitable team members, the best method is to involve the entire team in the interviewing process. Have every available team member interview every candidate. Then ask all of those who did the interviews to participate in the hiring decision. Not only will you make more informed judgments about the candidates, but the team members will have a stake in helping the new members fit in and become productive.

For recruiting from within the organization, the team members will likely know more about the candidates than you could possibly find out, so listen carefully to their comments. While they will be relatively relaxed in commenting about people from outside the organization, they will be less direct when discussing fellow employees. The best approach is to treat any hesitancy or uneasiness as a sign of potential problems. In addition to asking your team members, talk to the candidate's prior managers and associates. Previous managers from within your organization will generally be helpful. However, current managers are sometimes less honest, particularly if this is a troublesome employee who they are trying to get rid of.

For outside candidates, check every reference for signs of problems. Unfortunately, this is not foolproof. The only way to get honest references is by talking with previous coworkers. However, unless you know the references personally, most of them will be so concerned about possible litigation that they will not say anything negative. I have learned that the only way to detect potential problems is by the absence of strong positives. In this highly litigious world, you will rarely hear negative comments from any outside reference, even from someone you know.

My worst experience with a misleading reference was for a candidate who was highly recommended by someone I knew personally. After we had hired him, we found that he was almost impossible to work with. He insulted his teammates, made disparaging comments about their work, and refused to work cooperatively with anyone on the team. We were all surprised, since this behavior was totally different from what we had observed in the team interviews or learned from the references. While it took a while for this employee to do something so bizarre that we could dismiss him, he had learned to hide his flaws so well that they could not be discovered until after he had joined the group. In another case, in hiring an employee for a job that required a security clearance, a close friend gave the candidate a very strong reference without mentioning that he was a convicted felon. Needless to say, this made it hard to get the needed security clearance.

Difficult people are often very smart and have usually learned that they do not work well with other people. To get hired, many of these difficult people will be able to conceal their problems. While most people are straightforward and honest during interviews, some are not. For the most difficult people, interviewing is a highly intuitive process where you try to discover clues about how these people will behave on the team.

## 5.6 THE POWER OF COACHING

Most of us understand coaching and its purpose because of our early experiences on athletic teams. Although few of my early coaches were especially memorable, Coach Umbach was truly amazing. He wasn't a particularly impressive guy: only about 5 feet, 6 inches tall and 158 pounds. But no matter how big you were, if you ever got on a wrestling mat with him, you would never forget it.

Throughout my high school education, I had enjoyed sports but was never much good. This was frustrating because I was willing to practice and work out, but somehow my natural talents did not include ball games. My dad had been a wrestler in college and had enjoyed it, so when I got out of the Navy and went to college, he urged me to try out for the wrestling team. Since I was the only light heavyweight who tried out, I made the cut and was told to show up for practice. As we waited for the coach the next day, I got to know my teammates and it turned out that none of us had ever wrestled before. No one knew what wrestling practice involved or that coach Arnold W. "Swede" Umbach was a truly extraordinary coach.

When the coach arrived, we started with a brief warm-up and then a two-mile run, with the coach in front. Then he paired us up and had us work on a few basic holds. The coach took turns wrestling with each of us. After an hour and a half, when we were all pretty beat, we ended with another two-mile run, again with the coach in front. The workouts were so tough that the matches seemed easy. By the end of the year, several of us were undefeated, the team took the 13-state championship, and we were campus heroes. All of this from a ragtag bunch of inexperienced recruits. It was Coach Umbach who made the team.

Our coach's dedication, commitment, and energy were amazing, but what I found most inspiring was that he really cared about how each of us did. I have always remembered how he made a small band of raw recruits into a championship team and how he fostered the kind of cohesive team spirit that made losing simply unthinkable. I remember on my second match, after completing the regular three rounds, I was laying flat on my back, so exhausted that I knew I couldn't even get up for the final two tie-breaker rounds. All I could hear was Coach Umbach whispering in my ear that the other guy was every bit as beat as I was. All I had to do was get in there and "explode." To this day, I don't know how I did it, but I did, and I won.

## 5.7 TECHNIQUES FOR GETTING ALL TEAM MEMBERS INVOLVED

On most teams, there are a few experienced developers and several who are relatively new and inexperienced. The newcomers are often unsure of their roles, so they are reluctant to speak up or to voice opinions. If you let them, they will just watch. However, these silent members will not really be part of the planning process, the team will not get the benefit of their judgment, and the team will not have their full commitment at the end. Overcoming the team members' reticence and getting them all involved can take a great deal of effort and patience. Some techniques that can help are

- Ask, don't tell.
- Play dumb.
- Frequently check for agreement.
- Sense unspoken concern or disagreement.
- Don't let anyone monopolize the discussion.
- Manage the experts.
- Coach the team leader.

- Keep the focus on facts and data.
- Allow no observers.

### Ask, Don't Tell

Try to get everyone involved in all of the team discussions. One way to do this is to ask leading questions. For example, in defining the team's process, ask the members what they would expect to do first, and then second, and so forth. This will be hard at first, but the developers will soon loosen up and start contributing.

Keep asking and probing. For example, when a design is to be completed, ask about what should come next. Should they inspect the design, review the design with the customer, or start test planning? Bring up relationships with other groups such as hardware, systems, or test, and make sure that the team considers various ways of doing the job. Most products are designed in parts, so think about prototypes, multiple versions, or incremental builds. Ask how many parts there will be, the order in which they will be designed, and the sequence for their implementation and test.

Walk the team through each step in the development process. To truly represent what the members will do, the process must consider the many details and relationships that are likely to be forgotten during the job. Only then will the process be useful for detailed planning, and only then will it be used while the developers are doing the work. When everyone is included in developing this process, it will incorporate their ideas and be most likely to meet their needs. The team is then most likely to follow it.

While this sounds fairly easy to do and you will quickly learn to do it, the launch process is actually much more complex. Your objective is not a one-shot launch experience but a major behavior change. You want the team leader and all of the team members to learn how and why to involve every team member in the launch process and in all other important team activities. Only then will they continue to involve all their members in the key strategy, design, and planning decisions that the team will make every week.

## Play Dumb

When the coach is an expert on the subject the team is addressing and the team members know this, it is often difficult to get them to participate. For example, in defining the team's process, Fred was the organization's process expert. He was the coach and he was leading the team through defining the project process. He knew a great deal about the organization's process, and everyone recognized him as the expert. When Fred asked about the process they would use, none of the developers said anything. After a few moments, he started to write down a proposed process as the suggested starting point. He was the only person talking, however. No one agreed or disagreed; they just watched.

This approach is a mistake. At the end, Fred might get a very sound process, and it might even be an excellent process for the team to use, but it would have been Fred's process, not the team's. The objective is to get the team members to think through how they will do the job. During the team launch, the team members select standard roles, and one of these roles is the process manager. Fred should have had the team's process manager lead the process discussion. Then he should have guided the process manager in asking questions until the team produced a suitable process. This approach is important because, unless the process manager involves everyone in contributing to the process, it will be the process manager's process, not the team's. Unless the team members believe that they have the right process, they will not use it, at least not consistently. Without a sound process, the team's plan cannot be very good, and if the plan is not very good, the members won't follow it in doing the work. Under these conditions, the team members will continue working much as they have in the past.

Think about the process this way: What you want is a process that will work for this job, not a standardized framework that was defined by someone else. For example, there are now many organizations that have fully defined processes and many would be willing to give you a copy. Suppose you got a copy of such a defined process and gave it to the team. Would that be useful? Probably not. While there would probably be useful things to emulate in this process, the real need is to have the team members think through the work they plan to do, debate each step of the job, and then agree on how to do it.

The members need to do this before they produce the plan. If they don't, they will get so involved in estimating that they will not think through how to do the work. While they might get a reasonable estimate, the tasks will be in big chunks and many steps will not be defined. Such plans do not provide much help in doing the work. A defined process specifies how the work is to be done. Once the process is defined, the products named, and the product sizes estimated, it is relatively easy to estimate how long it will take to do each step of the process, particularly when the developers have historical data on similar work.

### Frequently Check for Agreement

Watch the team and notice who is talking and who is not. When someone has not said anything for a while, ask for his or her opinion and get the team leader and anyone else who is leading the team discussion to do the same. Don't make the question threatening by asking for specific answers like, "How big do you think this is?" Instead, ask what this person thinks. While you might expect the quiet types to duck the question and not give much of an answer, you will almost always be surprised. These are very bright people, and just about every time I have asked a quiet team member for an opinion, I have been surprised at how much he or she had to contribute.

So watch for the quiet ones. Frequently they are quiet because they are listening and thinking. They often have a good deal to say when given the chance. It almost always will be pertinent, and it will frequently be an important and useful contribution. But even if they have nothing new to add, just asking their opinion will help to get them involved. Help the team to treat every contribution with respect and to make the contributor feel good about having spoken up. Then, after you have asked them a few times, they will generally start to speak on their own.

After the first day or two, the team leader and some other team members should start asking each other for agreement. If they don't, discuss the subject with them and have them take responsibility for getting everyone's agreement.

### Sense Unspoken Concern or Disagreement

Another useful technique is to watch for disagreement. While some members will be outspoken when they disagree, others will indicate that they have a problem by an expression or some other nonverbal signal. Examples would be frowning, pushing away from the table, or acting nervously. While these signals are generally subtle and you have to watch for them, they are almost always detectable. After all, they are really signals and they are meant to be received. So, you can invariably tell when silent members disagree just by how they act. In such cases, ask a question such as, "Barbara, what bothers you about this?" Barbara will invariably have a good answer, and it will often be something that nobody else has thought of.

Another way to tell when there is disagreement is that nobody volunteers. For example, while one TSP team was reviewing its support plan in launch meeting three, the coach suggested that someone check with the other TSP teams to see what support tools they were using. The idea was that this would suggest useful tools for this group to consider. When none of the team members volunteered to do this, the team leader was about to assign someone. However, the coach interrupted to ask the members if there was some reason that his idea wouldn't be helpful. They were clearly reluctant to tell the coach that he had made a dumb suggestion, but one finally explained that this was a C++ team and that the other teams were all using Java. None of their tools could be used by this team. When developers on a self-directed team agree that an issue is important, someone will invariably volunteer to handle it. When no one volunteers, find out why.

## Don't Let Anyone Monopolize the Discussion

Occasionally, a team will have one member who talks more than anyone else. He or she is invariably the first to break in with a comment that turns into a monologue. The monologues then often drag on without adding measurably to the subject at hand. This situation can be difficult to handle for three reasons. First, neither you nor the team leader should be heavy-handed and autocratic in controlling the meeting, since that will destroy the informal and freewheeling environment required for team participation. It is also likely to cause everyone else to think twice before opening their mouths. Second, it is important to cut the monopolist off because he or she is wasting precious time, but do it diplomatically to avoid upsetting the rest of the team. Third, this person is a member of the team and his or her contributions and commitment are important.

You or the team leader can deal with such people either overtly or subtly. The overt approach is to use the rest of the team to help. When this speaker (say, Jed) has just finished a point and is about to continue, interrupt and say, "Jed, thanks, but before you go on, I would like some other opinions on this." Then return to the subject that the team is addressing and ask specific team members for their views. When Jed tries to break in again, politely say you are not done yet and ask another team member for his or her views. Let Jed speak from time to time, but break in periodically, either to get other opinions or to return to the subject at hand.

Often, these "Jeds" do not stay on the subject, and it is relatively easy to say, "Jed, thanks. While you have a point, we need to continue with the process. Let me write your point on the board and we can return to it later when there is time." Then write down the idea on a list at the side of the room and get on with the launch process.

Another and more subtle approach is nonverbal. As you or the team leader lead the discussion, walk around the room. If you are effectively leading the meeting, everyone will be talking with you and not holding private discussions. Thus, people will have trouble talking without making eye contact with you and being recognized. By standing directly behind Jed, he will have trouble talking without twisting around. This not only makes it difficult for him to talk, it makes it difficult for the rest of the team to hear him. Under these conditions, it is relatively easy to make eye contact with the other team members and ignore Jed without seeming to be impolite.

Above all, don't lose the Jeds. They are team members, and they frequently turn out to make valuable contributions. Usually, they just have some insecurity that makes them crave attention. Be polite and do not turn them off, for they can be helpful.

In fact, you can sometimes convert them into assets by asking for their help, possibly as the meeting recorder, for posting notes, or in maintaining a list of open questions and issues.

### Manage the Experts

Experts generally have information that the team needs. The problem is that just one expert can seriously hinder team communication. Much like Jed, the experts will have opinions on many topics, but they often do not have the patience to listen to other people's views.

One expert, Derrick, had been invited to help the team understand the planned product's technology. When he arrived, he opened with the comment, "Unless you have delivered a major project, you can't really know anything." Of course, this was a direct slap at almost every member of the team. While the team was largely composed of junior people, they were very bright, many had advanced degrees, and most had several years of experience. Not surprisingly, Derrick was not interested in anyone's views and he quickly antagonized the entire group. The coach soon broke up the meeting and reconvened later without Derrick. The group then quickly completed their conceptual design, but they had not been able to capitalize on Derrick's considerable experience.

Experts are often difficult to handle and you may have to occasionally treat them as Jeds. When these experts are members of the team, you cannot exclude them from the launch meetings or other team activities. One approach is to try to get the expert to help you handle the problem. Find a convenient time to have a private chat and ask for help. Point out that, as the expert, the rest of the team is likely to treat his or her opinion as the last word and feel unqualified to make further comments. Ask the expert to hold back and not state opinions too soon. Emphasize that while you need his or her views, you would appreciate getting them *after* the rest of the team has had a chance to speak. By taking a positive approach, you will usually get the expert's cooperation.

For example, in estimating and planning sessions, it is often possible to focus the expert's comments on how a product might work or what similar products the organization has developed. Then, get the team members to be the first to state size estimates. The principal problem is that the expert often will be outspoken on his or her views about the size estimate. Try to get other opinions, but don't turn off the experts. After all, they could be right.

If the experts are not team members, it is generally a good idea to keep them out of the working meetings. Start by having them meet with the group, state their views, and answer questions. Then let them leave with profuse thanks. Not only will this permit your team to jell as a working group, it will actually flatter the experts and save them the annoyance of sitting through long meetings and listening to people whose opinions they do not value.

You might also ask the experts to look over the team's final strategy, process, or design and to make comments or suggestions. Do not ask for comments on the team's plan, however, for experts are usually technical experts and not planning experts. They tend to make bad estimates, just like everybody else. In fact, they often feel that complex products are a lot simpler than they really are and they will tend to bias the team estimate to be much smaller than it otherwise would be.

Finally, experts are not always difficult, and some can be downright charming. In graduate school, I once went to a seminar where another student was describing his research work. Harold Urey, the Nobel Prize-winning chemist, came into the room and sat next to me. All conversation stopped until Professor Urey said, "Please continue." The speaker continued and Dr. Urey occasionally asked a question. It was soon clear that the professor was genuinely interested in what was being discussed and was there to learn. By this time, the speaker had gotten over his initial shock and the meeting continued. We were all enormously impressed. I have always felt that this was the best example of expert behavior I have ever seen. Most experts are very nice people and many are quite modest about their accomplishments, so don't hesitate to use them whenever you and the team think they could be helpful.

## Coach the Team Leader

While most team leaders will participate in the process along with the other developers, some cannot help acting like managers. As with experts, team leaders can end up dominating the team meetings. For example, Otis was leading his team during load balancing. All of the developers had completed their detailed plans for the next phase and several of them had much more work than they could possibly do in the available time. However, several others had relatively little to do. Otis was very concerned, so he immediately jumped up and started reassigning work among the developers. As he tried to mastermind the workload for the entire team, the developers just sat and watched. This was a large team and it was soon clear that Otis did not know enough to assign every task.

At this point, the coach suggested that they take a break. Then he met privately with Otis and suggested that he tell the team the basic schedule requirements for the load balancing work. Then the two of them would step out of the launch meeting and allow the team to do the load balancing. Otis agreed and, after the break, he told the team what was needed and said that he wanted to meet separately with the coach. The team members all participated in the load-balancing process and soon had a balanced plan that they all understood and accepted.

### Keep the Focus on Facts and Data

One important reason to use data is to make sound team commitments and to convince management that the team has a sound and aggressive plan. Also, a focus on facts and data will increase team member involvement. It levels the playing field. While experts will have lots of opinions, they rarely have a monopoly on the facts. By emphasizing the importance of data, you make it clear that no one knows all the answers and that everyone is equally capable of providing useful input. When the team members realize that one fact will trump a dozen expert opinions, the estimating process becomes less threatening, and the less experienced members are more likely to participate.

### Allow No Observers

There are three problems with having outsiders observe the launch process. First, they inhibit the team's discussions. Second, the observers may participate in the launch when they should not. Finally, the observers could react prematurely to the team's plan.

Carl's team was involved in a large system project and several groups insisted on participating in the launch. The manager of the requirements groups had several people working on this project, so he decided to personally represent his function. Similarly, the test manager had not yet assigned people to the job, but he had to plan the testing workload and needed to be involved. The process group manager also asked to be there because her people were fitting the TSP process into the organization's standard process and needed to understand how it worked. Finally, the quality assurance manager argued that with all of these other groups represented, it was unreasonable to exclude him.

When the team met to discuss goals and select team roles, there were more observers than team members. The coach started by asking the observers not to talk. They were quiet while the coach explained the meeting procedure and while Carl reviewed management's stated goals. However, when Carl started to discuss the customer's desires, the requirements manager interrupted to clarify several points. As the meeting progressed, the observers spoke up whenever they felt that the team had made a mistake or needed guidance. The bulk of the discussion during this launch meeting was among the team leader, the coach, and the observers. The developers remained pretty quiet and spoke only when they were asked to. Even if the observers do not talk, their mere presence will inhibit team discussion. It will then be almost impossible for the team to communicate freely and openly. Until the team members start to communicate freely and openly and to take positions and negotiate disagreements, the team cannot jell.

A more subtle message that observers send is, "We don't trust this team to work without management oversight." This problem is illustrated by the example of Peter's project. This team had started on the job before the TSP launch. The final delivery date had already been committed, and management insisted that the date was not negotiable. Peter and his team had decided to introduce the TSP, and everybody had been PSP-trained. When the launch was about to start, management insisted on having some representatives observe the launch process.

The launch started properly and the management observers didn't say anything. Most of the developers were initially reluctant to speak up, but the coach finally got some of them to contribute.

The team got through the conceptual design and size estimates with little trouble, but the size estimate turned out to be substantially larger than previously planned. Next, the team started on the total estimate for the overall job. They first estimated the remaining requirements work and then the high-level design tasks. Then they started to estimate the detailed design phase. When the team broke for lunch, it was clear that the early project phases would take much longer than management had expected.

During lunch, the observers met with the program manager and told him what they had heard. He then called in Peter, the team leader, and told him to abort the launch and to continue the project according to the original plan. While the management observers had not interrupted during the launch meeting, they could see where the launch was headed, and they judged that the team's plan would probably be unacceptable. Even before the team had finished planning, management reacted to the assumed plan and canceled the launch.

What is most interesting about this story is that the team did finish the detailed design when they had estimated, and they did follow their PSP practices while doing their work. At the end of detailed design, they were several months behind management's schedule. Management was in a panic, but the developers' work was of such high quality that they finished coding and testing much faster than management had expected. The team actually delivered the product ahead of schedule. Without the observers, the team would have had the time to produce a complete plan and to show management how they could spend more time in the design phase but still complete the job on schedule.

Since the story had a happy ending, you might think that this behavior didn't really cause any problems, but it did. According to the original plan, the design was to be done in December when a customer design review was planned. If the team met this review date, there was to be a substantial bonus payment. If management had known that the design would not be completed until April, they could have either renegotiated the design review date with the customer or arranged for the team to produce some early higher-level design documents in time for the December review. Since the developers didn't know about management's problems, they could not help solve them. Management forfeited a substantial award fee and as a consequence considered the TSP project to have failed.

## 5.8 PUT TEAMS TO WORK DURING THE STORMING PHASE

Jeff's team is a good example of the storming phase. When he and his team gathered after the opening management meeting, the only people in the room were the coach, the software and hardware development team members, and Jeff, the team leader. There were no other managers and no observers.

Several developers immediately started to argue with the coach. A similar previous project had taken two years and been a disaster, so the nine-month date was clearly impossible. Another developer objected to making a plan. "We don't even know the requirements, so how can we possibly make a plan?" Others were concerned with the launch schedule. "Without data, how can we possibly make a plan in only four days?" The coach took the time to address each of these issues.

First, he asked what management meant when they said that the job had to be finished in nine months. No one answered. The coach then asked what would happen if they produced the product in six months? Would management accept it? They all agreed that they would. Then he pointed out that what management really had said was, "We want this job done as fast as possible, and the fastest we think you can do it is nine months." They all agreed.

Next, the coach asked how long they thought the job would take. "After all," he pointed out, "in most negotiations, people don't usually accept the first bid. Management has made an initial nine-month bid. Now you should make a counteroffer. However, if you merely guess at a date, you won't be able to defend it. Then management will insist on their own nine-month guess." He told the team members that they must produce a plan that they could defend. If the plan was longer than nine months, they would know why and be able to defend it.

The team members again objected. "How can we make a plan when we don't even know the requirements?" The coach responded with another question. "You do have to make a commitment, don't you?" They agreed that they did. "Then you had better make a plan. You can't make a realistic commitment without a plan to meet that commitment."

The developers then argued that they could not make an accurate plan. Most of them were new to the job, and many had just joined the company. They didn't have any historical data, so they could not possibly know enough to make an accurate plan. The coach responded that a plan will always be more accurate when you have more information about the job. For maximum accuracy, the best time to produce the plan is at delivery time. Then they would know the most about the job, but then they would least need the plan. Right now, their plan would necessarily be inaccurate, but *now* was when the team most needed a plan.

The team's final argument was that they didn't have time to make a good plan. "How can we possibly make a plan in just a couple of days?" The coach asked how long it would take to make a good plan if they had historical data. They agreed that, under those conditions, planning would not take very long. "Now, without data," he asked "what do you have to do?" The developers thought for a few minutes, and one of them answered, "Guess." They all agreed that it should not take very long to guess. Then the team got to work to make a plan.

The key to coaching teams during the storming phase is to let the members vent their anger and frustration, then deal with their concerns. Don't rush teams through this phase, but help them understand and address their frustrations. Once they see that they have no choice and that the problem will not go away, they will agree to produce a plan. Once they do, they will want to get started right away.

The pressure to get to work will be greatest if the developers know that they will have to work into the evening whenever the launch falls behind schedule. The general guideline is to tell teams that, in the TSP launch, they work half days: from 8:00 AM until 8:00 PM. If they get right to work, they will likely finish early. Then they can leave at a reasonable hour!

The most effective way to move teams through the storming phase is to put them to work solving problems rather than just complaining about them. The TSP launch is designed to do just that.

## 5.9 BUILDING THE MANAGEMENT TEAM

Welding a group of ambitious, contentious, and aggressive managers into a cooperative and effective team is not easy. The first step is to respect the views of the team. When a decision affects their department, the team should be involved from the outset. Their views should be carefully weighed, even when it is known in advance that they are opposed. Any disagreement should be openly discussed, all the issues considered, and the key alternatives evaluated before a decision is made. Open debate enables managers to understand the issues and explain the conclusions to their employees.

Another advantage of involving team members in decision making is that it enables the managers to recognize new issues when they are raised by their people. If the issues were not considered during the decision making, the managers can reopen the discussion to ensure a more complete evaluation. It is surprising how often the professionals will see problems that their managers had not considered. Such reassessments can cause changes in the plans and produce better final results. By ensuring that all affected managers are part of the decision making, the organization can better utilize the knowledge and creativity of its people.

Although it is important to have all the top managers sit in on all key decision meetings, this alone will not build an effective management team. True participation requires active involvement, and the environment must encourage debate and contention. When everyone agrees, even experienced and capable managers are reluctant to object. It takes enormous self-confidence to voice the lone counter-opinion, but speaking up is the necessary first step in preventing serious mistakes. If senior managers truly want to understand their managers' views, they must provide an environment where everyone feels comfortable raising questions and voicing disagreements.

The final step in management team-building is to encourage management team members to work together. One senior manager did this effectively when he learned that his previously approved department budget had to be cut by $800,000. The division plan was being completed, and an error had been found in the departmental totals. The plan was too expensive and all departments had to make cuts to bring it into balance. Since the senior manager's budget cut was only about 3 percent, he was tempted to arbitrarily reduce everybody's budget by the same percentage. His people had worked hard to put together the plan, however, so he was reluctant to be arbitrary.

He called his top managers together, explained the situation, and emphasized the futility of an appeal. He was willing to make an arbitrary cut but wanted to see if his managers had better ideas. In the ensuing discussion, they each proposed cuts in other departments' budgets but none from their own. The senior manager finally concluded that he would have to make the cut himself, but offered to leave them for an hour to see if they could work out a better answer. None of them knew what the senior manager would cut, so they spent the next hour reassessing their priorities. They finally concluded that one major project should be completely eliminated and two others delayed, with the rest of the plan left as before. After they explained why they had decided on this new plan, the senior manager agreed with their proposal.

When the management team works together openly and honestly, it invariably produces the best results. These are generally the most capable and best informed people in the organization. They, as a group, are best able to balance technical and business issues and decide on sound plans of action. When they understand the decisions, believe they are right, and can defend them to their people, the professionals will know that their needs have been considered and are most likely to work energetically on implementation.

## 5.10 THE ESSENCE OF RATIONAL MANAGEMENT

With a rational management style, you have precise data on the organization and can make sound and timely decisions. Figure 5.2 shows the four elements of rational management. They are all related and are all required for an effective management style.

First, in setting product or operational goals, examine current performance and devise goals to meet business objectives. Then translate these long-term objectives into short-term goals that motivate action.

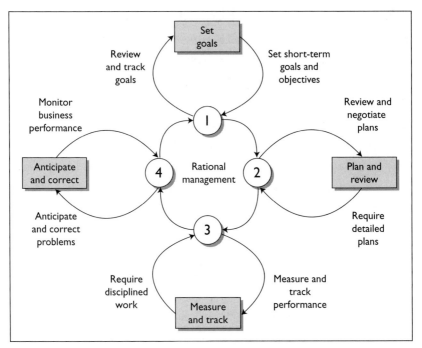

**Figure 5.2** Four elements of rational management

Second, require plans to meet the short-term goals. Goals drive plans and the people who will do the work must make these plans. Then have the engineers defend their plans and show you that they are complete and sufficiently detailed to guide the work. If a plan does not meet your goals, negotiate that plan to arrive at one that will meet your business needs and that the engineers will commit to meet. To work this way, the engineers must know how to make plans and they must be required to do so.

Third, measure and track the plans and monitor the discipline with which the work is done. Once you have a plan, you have a benchmark for measuring performance. To have any chance of meeting their commitments, however, the engineers must follow their plans, measure their work, and regularly report on their progress. This requires that they be trained in disciplined practices and that they measure and track their work and manage the quality of the products they produce. Then, of course, they must consistently follow these practices in doing the work.

Finally, continually monitor business performance. If you see problems, follow a rational management style to address those problems. When the work is planned, measured, and tracked, you can regularly monitor business performance. You will have a precise and timely picture of business status, and you can anticipate problems and take timely action to correct these problems before they impact business performance.

## SOURCES

**5.1:** From *TSP*[SM]*: Leading a Development Team*, Preface

**5.2:** From *TSP*[SM]*: Leading a Development Team*, Chapter 4

**5.3:** From *TSP*[SM]*: Leading a Development Team*, Chapter 4

**5.4:** From *TSP*[SM]*: Leading a Development Team*, Chapter 9

**5.5:** From *TSP*[SM]*: Leading a Development Team*, Chapter 6

**5.6:** From *TSP*[SM]*: Coaching Development Teams*, Introduction to Part I

**5.7:** From *TSP*[SM]*: Coaching Development Teams*, Chapter 4

**5.8:** From *TSP*[SM]*: Coaching Development Teams*, Chapter 2

**5.9:** From *Managing Technical People: Innovation, Teamwork, and the Software Process*, Chapter 18

**5.10:** From *Winning with Software: An Executive Strategy*, Chapter 3

# PART III
## Managing Your Boss

# 6
# Negotiating Your Projects and Defending Your Plans

**6.1 Projects Get into Trouble at the Very Beginning**
If you don't have a plan you believe is sound, make a new one and then negotiate a more realistic completion date with management.

**6.2 Keep Your Team Focused on Top Priorities**
Before agreeing to any change in direction, understand how it will impact the job.

**6.3 Always Make a Plan before Making Any Commitments**
Produce the best plan that you can, regardless of the pressure. Then defend it.

**6.4 Teach Your Manager to Negotiate With You**
Problems arise when your manager gives you a large change that you cannot contain by adjusting your current plan.

**6.5 Lean Really Is Mean**
When management eliminates support staffs, they do not understand that this will waste scarce and expensive software talent by forcing developers to do their own clerical work.

**6.6 What to Do When a Project Is Doomed**
Your best choice is to fix the problems before it is too late—but expect to be made the scapegoat.

**6.7 Autocratic Bosses Demotivate Workers and Diminish Performance**
A typical autocrat in effect says, "Let's compromise and do it my way."

**6.8 Is Your Environment Autocratic?**
The environment is autocratic if it produces unilateral plans with little or no team input.

**6.9 Building a Case for Process Improvement**
The biggest problem in starting an improvement effort is getting management support.

**6.10 Making the Strategic Case for Process Improvement**
You'll need to make a strategic case, because senior managers operate on the strategic level.

**6.11 Making the Tactical Case for Process Improvement**
When your managers are hypnotized by their short-term problems, you must focus on a few pragmatic steps that will fit their current priorities.

**6.12 What Management Expects from a Team Leader**
You are now expected to get work done by delegating to other people rather than doing it all yourself.

## 6.1 PROJECTS GET INTO TROUBLE AT THE VERY BEGINNING

Congratulations, you've just been promoted. You get to lead the new project we just won. You will have six engineers, but two of them are half time for a month or two. You can hire four more. The delivery date is nine months.

What do you say?

Most engineers would say, "Gee thanks, boss, I've always wanted to run a project and this sounds like a great opportunity. I'll give it my best shot, but the date looks awfully tight." If that's your answer, you lose!

Who owns the nine-month date? When your boss offered you the promotion, whose date was the nine months? It was the boss's date. But, when you said, "Boy that's a tough date, I'll do my best to meet it," whose date was it then?

Yours!

And don't ever forget it! You have just bought the ranch. Even though you had no intention of doing so, and you didn't even have time to think about it, bang, it hit you out of the blue. And there you are, the proud owner of a budding disaster.

So what else could you do? It turns out there is plenty you could do.

Projects usually get in trouble at the very beginning. They start with impossible dates, and nobody has time to think, let alone do creative or quality work. All that counts is getting into test, and the rush to test invariably produces a hoked-up product, a poor quality program, a late delivery, an unhappy customer, and disgruntled management.

While you can always say management was unreasonable, you will be responsible for being late and producing a poor-quality product. Everyone can easily blame somebody else, but do you really want to spend your life this way?

So you must take a stand. Most engineers are so focused on the job that they don't think about what the manager is saying. When managers say the delivery date is nine months, they are making a bid. And you bought it without a counter offer. You'd never buy a house or a car or a boat this way. You'd debate the number.

Think about it this way. Management has just said, "We have this key project, and the best date we think you can make is nine months." If you don't counter with another date, they will hold you to nine months. Unfortunately, if you just guess a later date, they will ask you why. And if you don't have a good answer, they will either ignore your date or get somebody who won't argue.

Management doesn't know how long the job will take, and neither do you. If you knew, and if you could convince them you knew, they would accept your date. If the project really will take 12 months, the last thing most managers want is a commitment to deliver in 9 months. You work for them, and they will also be held accountable for your schedule. They could easily lose their jobs if your project fails, and all you would lose is a chance to have another disaster. That would probably be a relief, at least after this project.

You must start by convincing management that you know how long the project will take. To do this, however, you must know yourself. This, it turns out, is not very difficult. It takes time and some hard work, but when engineers make careful estimates, and when they use historical data to make these estimates, they are generally pretty accurate.

The way you determine the date is to make a plan, and to make a very detailed plan. Since this can take a lot of work, and since you want your team to be part of this planning process, you need to get your new team to help you. This actually is the best possible approach. It will not only produce the best plan, but the team will then be in a far better position to do the work. They will also be committed to the schedule.

Then, when you have the plan, go back to management and tell them what the date really is. When they argue with you, as they will, take them through your plan. Show them as much detail as they will sit still for. Walk them through the *numbers*, and the *task lists*, and the *historical data* you used for comparison. Talk about *product sizes* and *productivity rates*. Show them enough to really convince them that you know what you are talking about.

Once you have made the sale, and management accepts your plan, stop selling and move on to the next subject. They will probably want to talk about alternatives. What would the date be with more staff, or reduced requirements, or a phased-version delivery plan? They may want you to present the plan to higher management, or to the customer. In fact, you will probably have to walk more people through the plan, so keep it dusted off, and make sure your backup is solid. Expect people to find any chinks or inconsistencies. Remember though, these are estimates. So tell them what you think and why, but remember that no one knows as well as you do how long the job will take.

If anyone can convince you that your estimates are off, be willing to make adjustments. As long as they have actual historical data to back up their opinions, and as long as these data are relevant to your project, consider the new facts. Under no conditions, however, make any such decisions on the spot. Any schedule change requires careful study and team agreement. So don't change your estimates without data and the time to review them with your team. Remember, almost all initial plans are tight, so don't cut your schedule without a very good story that the team agrees with.

So, when management says the date is nine months, the way to answer is to say, "That looks like a great opportunity boss. Let me get the team together and we'll take a look. We'll make the best plan we can, and be back to you in a couple of days."

If you think the schedule will be longer than management wants, don't argue about it right now. You don't have the ammunition to win that argument, and all that would do is convince management that you have a bad attitude. If they think you are out to prove their date is wrong, they won't let you make the plan. Remember, they don't believe you can give them a good date. After all, nobody has made good schedules before, so why should you be first?

So start with a positive attitude, and really drive for a better date. Give it an honest try, but then get the data to defend it.

## 6.2 KEEP YOUR TEAM FOCUSED ON TOP PRIORITIES

Your job is to keep your team focused on its top priorities. While Frank had not run a project before, he did a creditable job of forming and launching the team. Shortly after the launch, however, one developer proposed that they use a seemingly attractive new design method. Since everyone on the team agreed, Frank went along. The team then dove into the challenge of learning this better design method. Before they knew it, they had spent two months studying this method but had produced little actual product design. Since none of the team members had used this design method before and only two of them had taken any design courses, the developers had spent most of the last two months understanding the new method and deciding how to use it.

At this point, Frank reviewed the project with his manager. When he explained why they were so far behind schedule, the manager blew up. He told Frank to focus on building the product, not on learning a new design method. Since none of the developers yet felt competent with the new design method, the team decided to defer their design education and to revert to their earlier well-known and familiar design techniques. While this problem was caught fairly early in the project, the team had lost two months and never did recover. Even though the developers ultimately delivered a quality product, it was late and the project was never considered successful.

What should Frank have done? New processes, methods, tools, and practices can often help teams meet their primary goal. On the other hand, learning a new and unfamiliar method takes time. Unless you have professional guidance, it is usually a mistake to try new and unfamiliar methods in the middle of a project. However, if you decide that the benefits are worth the risk, make an introduction plan that includes professional guidance and allows time to learn and to become proficient with the new methods.

Frank should have told his team that they had a project plan that they must follow. If someone suggested a better way to do the job, he would gladly consider it, but he should have refused to change the design approach until he saw evidence that the new method would help the team and not expose their schedule. He should also have insisted that the team make a plan for adopting this new approach, and then he should have reviewed that plan with his management before making the change.

Taking a blind leap into some promising but unknown new method without prior experience, professional guidance, an introduction plan, and management agreement is invariably a mistake. Your top priority is this job. Before agreeing to any change in direction, understand how it will impact the job. This applies to all changes, whether in design methods, new tools, requirements enhancements, or anything else that is not in your current approved plan.

## 6.3 ALWAYS MAKE A PLAN BEFORE MAKING ANY COMMITMENTS

In almost any development organization, the developers are often pressured into making schedule commitments that they think are unrealistic. The problem is that the managers are also pressured by their executives and customers to meet aggressive commitments. Unfortunately, these managers typically think that the only way to manage development work is to give their projects a sense of urgency. Unless their staff are striving to meet an aggressive challenge, managers intuitively feel that their projects will not likely be successful. Therefore, managers will push until they are convinced that you and your teammates are striving to meet an aggressive plan. The problem we face as professionals is figuring out how to get management to accept a realistic plan. With the PSP skills and the TSP process, you will be able to do this.

Although most managers are reasonable, few have a sound basis for deciding what is a good plan. They may ask for a few expert opinions, but they will primarily depend on how you react when pressed. The proper way to deal with such requests is to *always* make a plan, even if management doesn't ask for one.

Say that you will do your best to meet management's goals but that you won't make a commitment without a plan. Don't say how hard the job is, that you think that a bigger team is needed, or anything else that might imply that you will not do your utmost to meet their requested date. Management has told you what is needed and you will do your best to do it, but you need a plan before you can commit to a schedule.

Only the dumbest managers want a flimsy plan that you can't meet. Managers have business commitments, and timely delivery is important. Product schedules are the foundation for revenue and expense projections. The managers may blame you for the current fiasco, but if they have too many fiascoes, they will lose their jobs. The most successful course for you and your team is to produce the best plan that you can, regardless of the pressure. Then defend it. In defending the plan, a generally successful approach is to stress the following points:

- This is the best plan we can make to meet the requirements you gave us. We can show you the plan assumptions and the historical data on which the plan is based and we can show you comparisons with similar projects. We think you will then agree that this is a tight but realistic plan.

- If you want to change the requirements or other assumptions, we will reexamine the plan to see how that will affect the schedule.

- This is a minimum-cost plan. If you are more concerned about the schedule, we could save time, but at added cost. We could also develop some schedule options if you can tell us what alternatives you would like us to consider.

You might even have alternative plans prepared in advance. The key points are to be responsive, to do a thorough job, and to make a plan before making *any* commitments. Examine any alternatives and do whatever you can to meet management's objectives, but resist any schedule or resource cuts that are not backed up with a plan.

This strategy works for individuals and for teams. With PSP training, you learn how to make a personal plan, collect data, and use data to manage and improve your performance. On a TSP team, the TSP coach will walk you through the TSP launch process and guide you and your team in developing the plan and defending it to management. This may sound risky and counter to your organization's culture, but it isn't hard when you use the TSP. Surprisingly, based on the experiences of TSP teams to date, it is *always* successful.

Having a sound and detailed plan is an important first step in maintaining project control. To maintain project control, however, you must follow the plan and keep it up to date. You must also keep management informed of your progress. Keeping the plan up to date is crucial because software development is a continuously changing business and every surprise usually means more work for you and your team. Although some of this change is a natural consequence of development work, the changes that are the hardest to manage are the ones that impact requirements scope and development resources. The key to managing such change requests is to take the time to update the plan and to explain to management what the change will cost. Then you must get management's approval for the cost, schedule, resource, and product impact before agreeing to the change.

This is not a question of blame but an objective way to explain the consequences of a proposed change. You had not planned to do whatever is now requested and it will take additional time and effort. Unless management and the customer are willing to accept the cost and schedule consequences, you cannot make the change and meet the original commitment. When you and your team follow this strategy, you will be surprised at how many changes turn out to be either unnecessary or deferrable.

Following the plan and keeping management informed are two aspects of the same issue. If you don't follow the plan, you won't know where you are in the project. Then you can't inform management of your status. If you can't keep management informed of project status, they will not trust you to run the project. Then you will face all kinds of uncontrollable pressures, such as scope changes, resource cuts, or special team-member assignments. Even worse, you won't have the plan to help you negotiate these changes with management. There are many ways that management can help, but they all require trust and under-standing. If you know where you are and if you keep manage-ment regularly informed, they will trust you and support you in maintaining control of your project.

Quality management is a major focus of the PSP and TSP because without effective quality management, the inevitable quality problems will impact your project's cost and schedule, and sharply reduce the value of your products. Although you may not be too concerned with the business value of your prod-ucts, you should be. Management hires and pays software devel-opers because the value of our products is substantially more than it costs to develop them. If your projects cost too much, then your products will cost too much and your customers could start looking elsewhere. If that happens too often, you could lose your job.

Teams are the most effective means humans have devised for doing complex creative work. Teams can be enormously effec-tive when they work properly; without adequate guidance and support, however, they can fail miserably. Team performance depends largely on the capability of the team members to work together. To be fully effective, teams must be properly formed, guided, and led. Unfortunately, in the development world, team formation, guidance, and leadership is largely a matter of chance. There is no teambuilding process, team leaders are rarely trained in effective leadership methods, and there is little or no team coaching. As a result, software teams are rarely as effective as they could be.

## 6.4 TEACH YOUR MANAGER TO NEGOTIATE WITH YOU

The most difficult form of management resistance concerns control. What makes this so difficult is that this type of resistance is almost always silent. Most managers have been promoted through the ranks and are now in positions of power. As working developers or team leaders, they had little control over resources, schedules, or priorities. Now they have the authority to make decisions and to give orders. They don't expect their people to argue or debate their directives but to obediently try to do what they are told.

When organizations adopt the TSP, these managers must deal with self-directed teams. Now, instead of merely doing what they are told, self-directed teams make detailed plans and negotiate the schedules. Instead of meekly trying to do what they are told, they argue and debate. This is a shock for managers who like the feeling of being powerful and in control. Instead of having orders instantly obeyed, they must now negotiate. Just as parents often have trouble adjusting when their children become argumentative teenagers, some managers do not readily adjust to self-directed teams.

There is no simple way to detect this control problem. One common symptom is when a manager assigns added tasks but refuses to let you make a plan for the new work. While each such change might seem too minor to debate, after several of these changes, your team's plan will no longer represent what it is doing. Then, without a realistic plan, you and your team can no longer assess the impact of the changes or negotiate schedule and resource adjustments. That puts your manager back in control and destroys your self-directed team.

One effective response to this tactic is to quietly make plan adjustments for every change. Instead of holding a relaunch or making a major replanning effort, make small plan adjustments every week. This will keep your plan consistent with the work and it will allow you to negotiate every change. While your manager may not like this response, you are merely being responsive to the requested changes by planning how to implement them. You will also still have a self-directed team.

Assuming that senior management continues to support your using the TSP, this strategy is relatively safe. The only problem is when your manager gives you a large change that you cannot contain by adjusting your current plan. Now you must decide when to face the music. Since your team is committed to the original schedule but you have now been given a change that will cause you to miss the committed date, you have a problem no matter what you do. While it is always tempting to delay the day of reckoning, the problem will not get better. The typical result of waiting is that you end up telling management about the schedule problem when it is unavoidable. Then management will blame you for the problem and you will have failed as a team leader.

Since such management behavior seems highly illogical and since managers are generally smart people, you might wonder why they would behave this way. There are many possible reasons. The most common situation is when these managers are unwilling to argue with their own manager. For example, if a marketing VP or a powerful customer demands a change that involves more work, the intermediate manager might not be willing to argue the schedule and resource case in front of senior management. Your best strategy in this case would be to suggest that your team present the impact story to the executive. While you could also lose the argument with the executive, the odds are that you will not. This, of course, assumes that you can defend your plan. Such a strategy would resolve your commitment problem and maintain your self-directed team.

If your manager refuses to let you make your case to senior management, try to find out why. While there are lots of possible reasons, the three most likely are that, first, your manager does not believe you have a very good story and is trying to help you. Second, he or she could be in some kind of trouble and does not want to raise any contentious issues with senior management. Third, it could be that senior management is really impossible to deal with and that your boss is trying to protect you. While there are lots of possible reasons for these escalation issues, you should first take the time to understand why your manager is behaving this way.

If he or she is really trying to help you, be careful to work with your manager and not at cross-purposes. If, however, you really conclude that your manager is being unreasonable, you only have three choices: you could go over your boss's head to senior management, you could do nothing and hope things will get better, or you could change jobs.

## 6.5 LEAN REALLY IS MEAN

Often our organizations pride themselves on having very small support staffs. An almost universally accepted management axiom is that overhead is bad and should be eliminated. In the resulting "lean and mean organizations," the engineers do their own clerical work. This is not an effective way to use scarce and expensive software talent.

By cutting overhead, management also eliminates the support staffs that the funds in the overhead budget support. While some of these groups are not the least bit interested in supporting the engineers, many are. Eliminating them can have enormous costs. Among these costs is the time every engineer must spend sorting through email, answering the phone, getting supplies, doing expense accounts, and filing mail and documents. In addition to the lost engineering time, this also means that most mail is not answered promptly if at all, phones go unanswered, supplies are wasted or overstocked, and little if anything is properly filed or can be quickly found when needed.

Perhaps most expensive and annoying, every software engineer in such lean and mean organizations must set up and maintain his or her personal computing environment. Just because we have the skills to do this doesn't mean we should. Most of us could repair our cars or paint our houses if we chose to, but it would take us longer than using someone who does this for a living. And we have other things to do. Why should we have to handle our own computing support?

The principal reasons that engineers spend less than half their time doing the tasks they were trained and hired to do is that, without adequate support, they have to support themselves. What is more, few engineers enjoy or are very good at being part-time clerks and technicians.

## 6.6 WHAT TO DO WHEN A PROJECT IS DOOMED

You're on a project and it's headed south. While everybody is trying their hardest, and you are doing your level best to help, you can feel it in your bones: the project is doomed to fail. What can you do? You have three choices.

1. Keep plugging away and hope things will improve.

2. Look for another job.

3. Try to fix the problems.

### Keep Plugging Away

While continuing to plug away is essential, it will not actually improve things, and it is not very professional. Often the best way to guarantee project failure is to keep working in the same way. Inertia is a form of surrender. You are acting helpless and hoping somebody will save the day, or at least hoping that the crash will not be fatal. So, plug away by all means, but do something else as well.

### Look for Another Job

Choice two is to look for another job, either in your current organization or elsewhere. This is always an option, and you should consider it if things get bad enough, but job-hopping has serious drawbacks. First, the situation in the new organization may not be much better—and it could be worse. Second, since projects often fail, you cannot continually run from failure or your resume will look like an employment catalogue. While this is not as serious a concern as it once was, it costs money to hire, orient, and train people. Unless management believes you will stay long enough to recoup their investment, they will not hire you. Third, changing jobs is disruptive and could involve a move and a new home. Once you have done that a few times, it loses its charm. Finally, in any organization, it takes time to become established and accepted. Until you are known and respected by management, you will not be considered for the best jobs. By moving, you start all over again at the bottom of the seniority list.

### Fix the Problems

Assuming that you don't want to give up, disrupt your life, or become unemployable, your best choice is to fix the problems before it is too late. Doing this, however, is tricky and it could actually damage your career if not done properly. Remember, the bearer of bad news often gets the blame. So if you are outspoken about the project's problems, expect to be made the scapegoat. This does not mean that you shouldn't act like a professional and try to fix the problems, just that you must do it very carefully.

Since you must deal with management to solve most project problems, try to put yourself in their shoes. Consider the problems they face and decide what you could do that would help. In doing this, you can safely make three assumptions.

1. Management already suspects that the project is in trouble.
2. They want solutions, not problems.
3. Managers do not want competition.

#### Management Already Suspects Trouble

Managers have lots of ways to get information, and the higher they are in the organization, the more sources they have. Managers also often develop a good intuitive sense and they can smell trouble even before anyone tells them. Once managers have worked with a few projects, the troubled ones take on a distinct character. The people begin to look worried and uneasy, the laughter and fun disappear, and status reports get vague and imprecise.

There are also various test, support, financial, and administrative groups that deal with most projects, and their people will hear of, or at least sense, the first signs of trouble. These people will almost certainly have passed on what they have learned to management and, if it is bad news, you can be sure that it will travel fast. So, management either knows about the problems already or has a strong suspicion.

### Management Wants Solutions, Not Problems

Busy managers have lots of problems. In fact, a manager's time is largely devoted to solving problems, whether generated by the projects, passed down from higher management, or imposed by the customer. If you go to your manager with another problem, expect to be greeted like the plague. However, if you show up with an offer of help instead, you will likely be received with open arms.

### Managers Do Not Want Competition

You have a manager who is responsible for your assignments, evaluations, pay, and promotion. If your manager sees you as supportive, you can likely get help in fixing the project. However, if your manager suspects you of competing for his or her job or thinks that you are out to get exposure to senior management, expect to get cut off at the knees. If your manager is experienced, you will not even know that you have been skewered until much later, if ever.

So, watch the chain of command and start with your immediate manager. Don't do anything your manager doesn't know about and agree with. While that doesn't mean your manager must know every step before you take it, be completely open and honest. Explain your approach, make sure you both understand the plan, and that you both agree on what you can do without prior approval. However, if the manager does not agree and you go over his or her head to a more senior manager, expect you or your manager to ultimately be fired.

If your manager agrees, he or she may let you carry the story upstairs, but most will do it themselves and you will not be involved or even get any credit. The key is to not worry about credit and visibility, but to concentrate on solving the problems. If you do that, sooner or later you will get plenty of visibility. There is a wonderful line by Dick Garwin, the designer of the first hydrogen bomb: "You can get credit for something or get it done, but not both."[1]

## 6.7　AUTOCRATIC BOSSES DEMOTIVATE WORKERS AND DIMINISH PERFORMANCE

Autocratic bosses are common. Starting with the construction of the early pyramids in Egypt, the literature is full of examples. Bosses have historically been slave drivers, demons with whips, or guards with guns. Historically, workers may have been slaves or prisoners, but that is not true of typical working environments today. However, in development work, bosses typically have very substantial power, and workers do not. This power confers a level of authority that bosses can use in autocratic ways.

Even when the boss is charming and seemingly respectful and friendly, that boss would still be an autocrat if he or she behaved unilaterally. Autocrats do not really consider the feelings or views of their workers. While this may sound extreme, it really is not. The true test is whether the boss actually considers your needs and views in making decisions. Merely pretending to listen to your opinions does not change the facts. A typical autocrat in effect says, "Let's compromise and do it my way."

Autocratic behavior is common because it can have substantial advantages for the autocrat. For example, autocratic decisions can be made quickly. Assuming that the autocrat is technically competent, this could be advantageous in dangerous situations

---

1. William J. Broad. 2001. "Who Built the H-Bomb? Debate Revives." *The New York Times*, April 24, D1.

like military campaigns or natural disasters. Autocratic behavior could also be effective when the autocrat-boss was better informed and more competent than the workers. This is often the case for simple and highly repetitive work. The autocrat can also get substantial personal rewards from unilateral action. Every time some autocratic command is promptly and successfully carried out, the autocrat's belief in his or her competence and infallibility is reinforced. This self-reinforcing characteristic of power led Lord Acton to say over 100 years ago that "power corrupts, and absolute power corrupts absolutely."

While this conclusion has been widely recognized and quoted, there is another similar conclusion that is not as well known: "Petty powers are most corrupting." Philip Zimbardo found this to be the case in simulated-prison experiments at Stanford University in the 1970s.[2] Zimbardo enlisted volunteers to act like prisoners and guards in a simulated prison. They had built a facility just like a prison in the laboratory basement and actually locked up the volunteer "prisoners."

What Zimbardo found was that, after only a couple of days, the "guards" started to behave so abusively that one of the "prisoners" actually had a severe emotional breakdown. He had to stop the planned two-week experiment in only six days. He concluded that ordinary people will often act in authoritarian ways when they are given even menial jobs that have some minor but absolute powers.

Zimbardo's conclusion can be seen in the behavior of many bureaucrats: they often tend to use their limited powers in arbitrary and highly authoritarian ways. This is what makes some

---

2. Malcolm Gladwell discusses Zimbardo's work on pages 152 to 155 of his book *The Tipping Point: How Little Things Can Make a Big Difference*, Little, Brown and Co., New York, 2000. The original reference is: C. Henry, W.C. Banks, and P.G. Zimbardo. 1973. "A study of prisoners and guards in a simulated prison." *Naval Research Review*, 30, 4-17.

clerks, guards, or other support people insist on strictly interpreting the rules although that interpretation would make no logical sense in the specific case at hand. This kind of strict adherence to work rules makes organizations unresponsive and hard to work with. It can also be expensive and demotivating.

There are four reasons for people to behave autocratically.

1. There is a crisis.

2. There is a power vacuum, and they feel they must take charge.

3. They act autocratically because that is the way such jobs have always been done.

4. They get emotional benefits from being autocratic.

**The Crisis**—In times of crisis, rapid decisions are often required, and a single authority is usually thought to be most effective. Most people understand and accept that this is the best way to behave in such cases.

**The Power Vacuum**—A power vacuum can occur in a crisis when the leader is either killed or otherwise unavailable and someone takes over. Such cases can arise in almost any situation, and it may be seen in combat when the commanding officer is killed, and a sergeant or even a private takes charge. While this situation need not lead to autocratic behavior, it generally does when nobody else seems willing to or able to make the needed decisions.

**Force of Habit**—While power vacuums can occur in development, the force-of-habit case is more typical. Development managers have generally managed in this way so pretty much everyone does. Furthermore, since it seems so natural and expected for the boss to make all of the decisions, force of habit tends to create power vacuums. Nobody but the designated boss feels able to make decisions.

**Emotional Reinforcement**—Emotional reinforcement presents an entirely different situation. When the person has clear authority and resists either suggestions or appeals to common sense, it is generally a good idea to keep quiet and do what you are told. If this person is your boss, it may not be clear whether he or she would accept suggestions or not. This is when you may have to conduct tentative tests to see how your suggestions are received. While I have only seen a couple of truly autocratic managers in 50+ years of development experience, they do exist, and they can be both unpleasant and threatening to work for, particularly if, like me, you like to make your own decisions.

While autocratic environments are not pleasant places to work, they can be reasonably efficient when the boss is both competent and fully capable of directing the work. Even in these cases, however, it has long been known that autocratic management styles demotivate the workers and produce less than optimum workplace performance.

One reason for this is explained by James Surowiecki in his book *The Wisdom of Crowds*.[3] He cites many examples of how groups typically make much better decisions than even expert individuals. This is particularly important for development groups and is the reason that autocratic behavior is ineffective and often even counterproductive. This is true regardless of how pleasant and friendly the autocrat is; the problem is unilateral behavior.

## 6.8 IS YOUR ENVIRONMENT AUTOCRATIC?

Since it is often hard to recognize that you are working in an autocratic environment, an example may help. In one case, a

---

3. James Surowiecki. 2004. *The Wisdom of Crowds: Why the Many Are Smarter than the Few and How Collective Wisdom Shapes Business, Economies, Societies, and Nations.* New York: Doubleday.

development team was starting a new project and management told the team leader that the job had to be completed in nine months. The team leader then produced an overall plan with key milestones for

- Design-specification sign-off
- Detailed design complete
- Code complete
- Functional testing
- System testing
- Customer-acceptance testing

He then met with the entire development team and reviewed his proposed plan. Over the next couple of hours, he answered all of the developers' questions and made some minor additions and adjustments to the plan. In the end, even though none of the developers felt that the nine-month schedule could be met, the team agreed to the plan pretty much as the team leader had originally proposed it. This team leader then told management that his team now had a plan to deliver the finished product in the desired nine months.

The question is: "Is this autocratic behavior?" Most developers would say no. This is how most of their projects have always been run. They believe that they could have spoken up and made changes to the plan if they had wanted to. Furthermore, most of them also felt that the team leader knew more about planning than they did, and they may even have believed that he or she had produced a better plan than they could have. Finally, since they had to meet management's nine-month schedule and this plan did, they didn't have anything better to suggest. The team leader would also likely argue that he or she was not being autocratic. After all, there was a full team review of the plan and all of the team's suggestions and changes were incorporated.

While it is true that this style is nothing like that of the despot or slave driver of old, it still results in a unilateral plan that was produced with little or no team input. While minor changes were made, the plan had the original resources management allocated, it produced the product that they had specified, and it met management's suggested end date. Such plans commonly have three important characteristics.

1. They do not guide the developers in doing the job.
2. They do not have the full commitment of the team members.
3. They are rarely met.

The next question, of course is: "If this is autocratic management, how else could you produce a plan?" The answer is to truly involve the team in making its own plan. However, there are typically two objections to doing this.

1. It would take too long.
2. The developers wouldn't know how to make a plan.

Of course, if you don't mind getting inaccurate and largely useless plans, it doesn't make much difference how you produce them. However, if you want accurate and useful plans, it might make sense to consider alternatives.

## 6.9 BUILDING A CASE FOR PROCESS IMPROVEMENT

Perhaps the biggest problem in starting an improvement effort is getting management support. The first and most important step is to get senior management backing. Without support from the very top, it is generally impossible to make significant changes. Next, however, you will need active involvement from all the appropriate managers, particularly those managers who directly supervise the work to be impacted by the change.

The reason for broad management support is that significant improvement programs generally involve substantial changes in the way people work. If you don't change the engineers' working practices, you can change the organizational structure and all its procedures, but nothing much will really change. Thus, to have a substantial impact on an organization's performance, you must change the way the engineers actually work. While this is possible, it is very difficult, and it requires the support of all levels of management. Senior managers must establish goals and adjust reward systems. Intermediate managers need to provide funding and change priorities. And most important, the working-level managers must make the engineers available for training, support process development, and monitor the engineers' work to make sure they follow the improved practices. So, how do you get this kind of support? There are three issues:

1. Why do you want to make changes?
2. Which managers do you need support from?
3. Why should those managers support you?

**Why Do You Want to Make Changes?**

You may be interested in making process changes, which may be changes in the way your organization develops or maintains software. This means you are probably talking about some kind of process improvement, like getting a Capability Maturity Model (CMM) program underway or introducing the Personal Software Process (PSP) and Team Software Process (TSP). Whatever the approach, you will be changing the way software work is done.

The first question to address is: why? That is, why do you want to improve the software process, why should management support you in improving the software process, and why should the organization care about how software is developed? These are tough questions, but they are the very first questions managers will ask. You need to be able to answer these questions, and depending on which managers you talk to, they will ask these questions differently. This leads us to the next question.

### Which Managers Do You Need Support From?

Depending on the size of your organization, there could be many management levels. Typically, the manager from whom most of us need support is the manager immediately above us. While there are lots of levels to discuss, let me assume that this immediate manager runs a project or a department. Unless you are in a very small organization, this manager probably works for some higher-level manager, and this higher-level manager probably works for some manager at an even higher level. Up there somewhere there should be a senior-level manager or executive who is concerned with the overall business, how it performs now, and how it will perform in the future. This senior manager is concerned with where the business stands competitively, how new technology will impact its products and services, and the changing needs of its customers.

The reason the manager's level is important to you is that improvement programs focus on long-term issues that are the principal concern of senior-level executives. Unless the managers below the executive level are specifically charged with working on process improvement, most of them will view improvement efforts as a distraction at best or, at worst, as a drain on critical resources.

The reason for this negative view is that process improvement deals with the overall performance of an organization. It concerns competitive capabilities, long-term cost effectiveness, development cycle-time improvement, and customer satisfaction. These are strategic issues that generally only concern the most senior executives. Even in the departments, laboratories, or divisions of large corporations, the performance measures for division general managers, laboratory directors, and department managers are invariably concerned with immediate short-term results: delivering products on time, managing tight budgets, or responding to customer-related crises.

While these issues are critically important, and they often spell the difference between organizational failure and success, a total concentration on these topics will not change the way organizations perform. If the organization is not cost competitive, or if it produces lower quality or less attractive products, a focus on current performance will not improve the situation. The immediate problems may be fixed and the burning issues resolved, but the organization will continue working pretty much as it always has. It will thus continue producing essentially the same results and generating essentially the same problems and issues. This brings us to the definition of insanity: doing the same thing over and over and expecting a different result.

Generally, only the managers who think strategically will support a process-improvement program. These are usually managers who have broad business responsibilities and are measured by total organizational performance. They probably have multiple functions reporting to them, like product development, marketing, manufacturing, and service.

Even senior managers, however, do not always think strategically. Most organizations, after all, are owned by stockholders who are interested in the stock price. And since the stock price is heavily influenced by quarterly financial results, even the most senior managers cannot afford to ignore short-term financial performance. Unfortunately, many of these managers don't worry about much else.

### Why Should This Manager Support You?

Now we get to the critical question: Why should any manager support you? In general terms, there are three reasons why managers might be willing to support you:

1. What you want to do supports their current job objectives.

2. What you want to do will make them look good to their immediate and higher-level managers.

3. What you want to do is so clearly right that they are willing to support you in spite of its impact on their immediate performance measures.

The relative importance of these reasons changes, depending on where the manager resides in the management chain. At the very top are the managers who are most likely to focus on long-term performance. This means that they will often support process improvement for all three reasons. Thus, if you can show that process improvement will have a significant long-term benefit, you will likely get support. You can generally accomplish this by showing how similar improvements have benefited other organizations or, better yet, how they have benefited other parts of your own organization.

For the CMM, for example, show how improvements in CMM level have improved the performance of other software organizations. Also, show where your organization stands compared with other organizations in your industry. For the PSP and TSP, you could show data on quality, productivity, or employee turnover and how such changes could impact your organization.

If you can get the attention of a senior manager, and if you have your facts straight, the odds are you can get this manager to seriously consider the subject of process improvement. Frequently this is when you might get an outside expert to give a talk or to do an assessment. While you may have to settle for a small initial step, the key is to get some action taken. Once you can get the ball rolling, it is usually easier to keep it in motion.

If the manager you are dealing with is not at the senior executive level but one level lower, this manager is probably not measured on strategic issues. Such a manager would know, however, that his or her immediate manager had such a measure. Thus, your manager is not likely to be motivated by reason 1 but might be persuaded to support you for reason 2. Thus, by proposing something that will make him or her look good to higher-level managers, this manager will personally benefit while also helping you to get the improvement ball rolling. What you want to ask for from this manager is help in taking the improvement story upstairs.

Finally, the most common problem is dealing with a manager who is fairly far down in the organization. This manager not only is not measured on strategic issues, but his or her immediate manager is not either. This means that strategic objectives are not likely to be very compelling. At this point, you only have two choices:

- Convince this manager that the improvement is a strategic necessity for the organization.
- Show how the improvement effort can help to address immediate short-term concerns.

While the latter is often the approach you must take, it has a built-in trap. The reason is that if improvement is aimed at solving a short-term problem, as soon as the short-term pain is relieved, the need for improvement is gone. This is like taking aspirin for a splitting headache. If the headache is indeed a transient problem, that would be appropriate. If the pain is the first symptom of a stroke or a brain tumor, however, the delay could be fatal. While promptly taking an aspirin may usually be helpful for a stroke, you had better also see a doctor right away.

In the software process, the problems in most organizations are more like strokes and brain tumors than they are like headaches. While you may have no choice but to sell the improvement effort as a short-term solution, try to move to strategic issues as soon as you can get the attention of someone upstairs.

## 6.10 MAKING THE STRATEGIC CASE FOR PROCESS IMPROVEMENT

So you've decided to approach management about a process improvement effort. If you can get the ear of a senior manager, then you'll need to make a strategic case, because senior managers operate on the strategic level. How do you prepare and what do you say?

The approach to follow for almost any type of improvement effort would be much the same:

- Clearly define what you propose.
- Understand today's business environment.
- Identify the executive's current hot buttons.
- Make an initial sanity check.
- Start the plan with two or three prototypes.
- Estimate the one-time introduction costs.
- Determine the likely continuing costs.
- Document the available experience data.

- Estimate the expected savings.

- Decide how to measure the actual benefits.

- Determine the improvement's likely impact on the executive's current key concerns.

- Identify any other ways that the proposed improvement could benefit the business.

- Produce a presentation to give this story clearly and concisely.

## Defining the Proposal

Before you do anything, define exactly what you want the executive to do. The best guide that I have found is to actually prepare an implementation letter for the executive's signature. Then in the meeting, if he or she says, "Great, let's do it," pull out the letter and hand it over as a proposed implementation instruction. While this reaction is not likely, the exercise will help you to produce a clear statement of what you intend to propose. Also, if you are several management levels removed from this executive, you should describe the letter as a proposed draft instruction that you have not yet reviewed with your immediate management. Better yet, show the draft letter to your manager first and get his or her suggestions on improving it.

## Understand Today's Business Environment

In preparing for the presentation, remember that there is no magic formula for convincing senior managers. Every case is different. The approach must vary depending on the situation and the executive's current priorities. If, for example, this executive has just cut resources to meet a profit goal or the organization has just lost a major contract, this might not be a good time to propose an additional expense. So, plan your improvement strategy with a clear appreciation of what is happening right now in the business.

## Identify the Hot Buttons

Next, find out what this executive is most concerned about. Since most executives give lots of talks and issue many statements and announcements, this is generally fairly easy to do. With few exceptions, executives use every available occasion to plug the topics they feel are highest priority. So get copies of some of this executive's recent announcements and presentations, and look at the common themes. You will usually see a fairly consistent message. The manager may frequently mention profitability, or market growth, or development cycle time. Because executives are concerned with many things, he or she will almost certainly make many points. But if there is an overriding concern, much like a television commercial, this topic will pop up every time there is an opportunity. Once you know the executive's current hot button, figure out how the process improvement you propose would address that concern, then make sure the improvement justification addresses this topic.

## Make an Improvement Sanity Check

In preparing an executive proposal, the first step is to gather the known facts about the costs and benefits of the proposed improvement program. As soon as you have the data, make an initial sanity check: Does the proposed process improvement directly address the executive's key concerns? If not, are the cost savings significant enough to justify the executive's listening to the proposal? If the improvement directly addresses something the executive has been pushing for, then cost will not be a key concern. If cost savings are important, however, are the proposed savings large enough to be convincing?

Most executives know that improvements are rarely as effective as first proposed and that there are always hidden costs. A good rule of thumb is that improvements with savings of two or more times are usually impressive while numbers below 25 percent are likely to be ignored or subjected to very close scrutiny. If cost is important and you are not proposing a significant cost saving, consider putting off the presentation until you can make a stronger case.

### Prototype Introduction

If the proposed improvement passes this sanity check, the next step is to analyze the costs of introduction. It is almost always a good idea to start an improvement program with one or more prototype tests. This not only reduces the initial introduction costs, it also maximizes your chances of success. Just about any change will affect both engineer and management behavior, and these changes are rarely natural or easy. Thus, many people will likely have initial problems following the new methods. To be successful, you must identify and resolve these problems at the very beginning. The longer it takes people to properly use the new methods, the more the introduction will cost and the longer it will take to show benefits. The principal advantages of starting with a prototype program are that the initial costs are lower and it is easier to watch a few limited pilot programs to make sure they are getting the needed support and assistance.

One major risk in any improvement program is that the prototype project could be cancelled or redirected. To protect your project from this risk, try to get two or three trial projects underway. That way, if one is killed or redirected, you will still have the others to fall back on.

### Introduction Costs

While you will almost certainly follow a gradual introduction strategy, it is a good idea to show both the prototype and the total introduction costs. The reason is that the introduction strategy will probably change several times before you are done and you don't want to keep changing the cost–benefit story. Emphasize that you are presenting the total introduction costs for the entire organization, but that the initial costs for the prototype program will be much lower.

In any significant improvement, there will be initial introduction costs as well as continuing costs for sustaining the improvement. Since any process-improvement introduction will require some executive and management time, you need to make an appropriate allowance. Generally, however, the major costs will be the time to train and support the engineers. Even the introduction of a new tool takes training and support, so don't gloss over the introduction costs; they can amount to very big bucks.

For example, with a new programming language, a minimum of two weeks of intensive training is usually required, often followed by a period of close consultation during initial use. Similarly, a new tool will require an initial training session of several days plus guided practice sessions and continuing professional support for at least a few weeks.

In estimating these costs, remember one key guideline: Your story will be judged by its weakest point. If someone finds an error or a serious underestimate anywhere in the story, the assumption will be that similar errors infect the entire story. So be careful about making low estimates or assuming that some costs are insignificant. If you don't know the facts, find someone who does. Above all, don't make unsupported assumptions; your entire presentation could be discredited.

In addition to executive, manager, and engineering time, trainers and expert assistance will almost invariably be needed. This can add a significant cost, particularly if you plan to use outside assistance. On the other hand, the costs of building internal experts and trainers can be very large, and few executives will want to make such a significant commitment, at least until the proposed improvement has been proven with early tests.

### The Continuing Costs

After the improvement has been introduced, there will be ongoing support costs. You may need continuing training to cover engineering turnover or staff growth. Expert assistance and support may also be needed. These costs can be substantial, so it is important to identify them. Describe them clearly up front and then justify them. If you don't give a complete cost story, management will sense that there are hidden costs and likely assume that these costs are much greater than they actually are.

### The Process-Improvement Benefits

Next, we turn to the benefits. Here, you must address two points: first, how long will it take for the improvement program to recover the introduction costs, and second, how will the improvement address the executive's principal concerns? If you can show that the improvement will pay for itself, then the other benefits would be pure gravy. So start by making the cost case.

The way to make the cost case is to first gather the available facts on improvement benefits. Here, you are at a disadvantage. Costs are always easier to prove than savings. Executives know this, however, probably better than you do. After all, they spend much of their time justifying changes. So don't worry about proving an ironclad case; executives will rarely demand it. But they will want a logical story that hangs together and looks complete and realistic.

### Improvement Experience

So, first, what are the available facts? Unfortunately, there are few statistically sound improvement studies, even for accepted process-improvement methods. While there may be some available analyses, you will probably have to rely on anecdotal evidence. This may not be as precise as a comprehensive statistical study, but such evidence can be even more convincing. The best case would be one in which someone in your industry has implemented the same improvement and described its benefits in a talk or a paper. If you can find a suitable example, summarize the general findings in the executive presentation, but then emphasize the results reported by your competition.

### Calculating the Savings

There are many ways to save money. In the final analysis, however, most software cost savings result from personnel reductions. For example

- By introducing a design inspection program, you can eliminate defects early in the process and save considerable rework.

- A measured quality program can reduce the number of defects found in test and shorten testing time.

- A configuration-management system can save development time by ensuring that correct program versions are always available.

- A change-control system can reduce the number of uncontrolled changes and save development time.

While these savings are all real, they all have the disadvantage of being very hard to prove, either in advance or after the fact. As a result, the most convincing argument is generally that the XYZ Corporation cut their test time by x percent, or that the ABC Company reduced customer-reported defects by y percent. Starting from these numbers, you can then generally show the amount of money you would save if your organization had similar results.

### Measuring the Benefits

In concluding the presentation, discuss how the prototypes will be designed to measure the improvement benefits. For example, if the proposed improvement is intended to reduce development cycle time, discuss how to demonstrate that it does. A common problem, however, is that few organizations have data on their current operations. Thus, even if you conduct a highly successful prototype experiment, you may have no way to show that it was successful. That is, you will have lots of "after" data but no "before" data with which to compare it. As part of the proposal, raise this issue and suggest ways to handle it.

Even when organizations have little or no data on their current operations, there are usually a few things that you can measure. For example, data are often available on the length of time by which projects have missed their planned delivery dates. There are also often records of the numbers of defects found in system test or reported by customers. Similarly, data can generally be found to calculate the percentage of the development schedule that is spent in integration and system test. Another good measure is the total development hours divided by the total lines of delivered source code. While no single measure can characterize the quality of an organization's processes, there are many possible measures that can be obtained from most accounting and project-reporting systems.

Because you need to apply these measures to the existing projects, it is important to start looking around for available data even before you make the proposal. Then you can use these data in justifying the proposed improvement. Also, you can be reasonably sure that there will be a way to measure the benefits when you are done.

### Other Benefits

While cost savings are important, not all improvements can or should be cost justified. For example, if you can show that the change will improve schedule accuracy and predictability, reduce cycle time, or make your organization more competitive, management will often approve the proposal, even if it does not clearly save money. The key is to convince management that the improvement is good for the business and then, if possible, show that it will also pay for itself. If you cannot prove the savings story, however, don't give up. If the other benefits are compelling, management may be willing to proceed anyway.

## 6.11 MAKING THE TACTICAL CASE FOR PROCESS IMPROVEMENT

In the typical organization, management claims to be thinking strategically. However, imagine that you work for a company in a highly competitive industry that is struggling to improve its quarterly earnings. While process improvement is accepted as a great idea, nobody will invest any significant money in it. What is more, the costs in your improvement proposal must be justified, and you must show that the costs can be recovered in less than a year without seriously disrupting any project.

Management claims that its goal is to be the industry leader, but the first question managers are likely to ask is, "Who else is doing this and what good has it done them?" While you might be tempted to suggest that they sound like followers instead of leaders, restrain yourself and try to think about how to justify this proposal in a way that management will buy. This is the situation. What can you do?

While management knows all of the buzzwords, would like to act strategically, and talks about being the industry leader, managers are hypnotized by their short-term problems. Either business realities will not permit a long-term view, or some higher-level manager is under severe pressure to show improved quarterly financial results. Under these conditions, you must ignore all the high-sounding phrases about leadership, quality, and improvement, and focus instead on a few pragmatic steps that will fit the current realities.

The only way to break through management's resistance is to somehow demonstrate that the organization's current short-term problems cannot be fixed with short-term Band-Aids. You must take a strategic view. The two principal approaches you can take are to (1) make the strategic improvement activities tactically attractive, or (2) start a small tactical effort and gradually build it into a strategic improvement program.

The U.S. Air Force's decision to evaluate bidders based on their process maturity made the Capability Maturity Model (CMM) process-improvement program attractive to many managers. The Air Force evaluations forced many tactically focused managers to invest in process improvement to avoid losing business. This illustrates the advantage of having a customer demand quality improvement: it makes strategic improvement programs tactically attractive.

This strategy will generally work when you have a customer that is interested enough in quality to require that its suppliers commit to improvement programs. If you have such a customer, you can often connect your process-improvement proposal to that customer's demands. If you can get the support of your marketing department, your chances of success are pretty good. While you must keep the scale of your improvement program realistically related to the size of the likely new business, if an important customer insists on a quality program, you probably have a sound basis for a process improvement proposal.

Another approach that is almost as effective is to connect your improvement efforts to an already approved corporate improvement effort. Examples would be obtaining ISO 9000 certification or initiating a 6-sigma software quality improvement effort. Again, if you can show that the improvements you espouse will assist the organization in meeting already established goals, you have a reasonable chance of getting the improvement effort approved.

If neither of these strategies work, you probably will not be able to make a strategic program tactically attractive, at least not in the short term. Under these conditions, you must focus on justifying a series of small improvement steps. You could identify one or two narrowly focused efforts that can be completed rather quickly and that don't cost a great deal of money. Then put them into place and use the resulting benefits to help justify taking the next step.

If you are careful about what improvements you pick, and if you build support for each step as you take it, over time, you can probably keep the improvement program moving forward. Then you can gradually convert your short-term tactical activities into a longer-term strategic effort.

The critical issue in this situation is getting approval for the initial effort, and then getting the engineers and project managers to support each step as you take it. As long as you can demonstrate that the program is not too expensive and is producing results, and as long as you have the support of the project managers and working engineers, you can probably keep the program going. Then, given a little time, you should be able to show that you are saving the company money and improving project performance. This should allow you to gradually increase the size of the improvement program.

In picking improvement efforts, concentrate on activities that are low cost, can be implemented by one or two projects, will produce immediate measurable results, and will attract strong project support. While there are several candidate improvement activities that meet these criteria, the ones that are probably the best bets for organizations at CMM levels 1 or 2 are code inspections, design courses, and the Personal Software Process/Team Software Process (PSP/TSP). These can all be focused on individual projects, and they all support various aspects of a CMM-based process improvement strategy.

Pick efforts that can be implemented without a broad organization-wide effort that requires senior management approval. Then, if the involved project leaders agree to support the proposal, management will generally go along. Because these improvement efforts can be implemented without requiring changes in the entire organization, they are good candidates for quickly demonstrating the benefits of process improvement programs.

Code inspections can be put into place quickly, and they pay enormous dividends. While design inspections could also be helpful, they take more time and money and don't have nearly as high a payoff unless you have an effective design process in place. Therefore, it is usually best to defer initiating design inspections.

To start a code inspection program, first find a project leader who agrees to implement the initial trial program, and then train all of the engineers who will do the inspections. In addition, get some member of your staff qualified to moderate the inspections and to help the engineers to do the inspections properly. It would also be advisable to hire an expert to teach the initial courses. In starting an inspection program, a number of available references can be helpful,[4] including Appendix C of my book *Introduction to the Team Software Process*, which describes the inspection process.[5]

After you complete the first code inspections, you can usually use the engineers who did them as references to help convince the leaders of the other projects. While it will take time to put a complete code inspection program in place, it will provide substantial benefits, and it should give you a firm foundation for further improvements.

Until code quality is reasonably good, design improvements generally will not improve test time or product quality substantially. The reason is that poor quality code will result in so many test defects that the design problems will be lost in the noise. However, once you have code inspections in place, you get substantially improved code quality and reduced test time. That is when design courses would make sense.

While it is almost impossible to justify the costs of a design course, you probably will not need to do so. Most people intuitively understand that design is important, and engineers generally will be interested in taking a design course. Start by identifying a project leader who is willing to sponsor the initial test, then find a qualified instructor and get some design courses

---

4. See the following for information on code inspections:

   Michael Fagan. 1976. "Design and Code Inspections to Reduce Errors in Program Development." *IBM Systems Journal* 15, no. 3.

   Michael Fagan. 1993. "Advances in Software Inspections." *IEEE Transactions on Software Engineering* SE-12, no. 7, July.

   Tom Gilb, Dorothy Graham. 1993. *Software Inspection,* Edited by Susannah Finzi. Reading, MA: Addison-Wesley.

   Watts S. Humphrey. 1989. *Managing the Software Process.* Reading, MA: Addison-Wesley.

5. Watts S. Humphrey. 2000. *Introduction to the Team Software Process*[SM]. Reading, MA: Addison-Wesley.

taught. Assuming that the course is of proper quality, other projects will want to join in, and demand for the course will grow quite quickly.

The only additional requirement is that you have one or two qualified people available to consult with the engineers and to advise them on how to use the design methods when they start applying them on the job. Then, after the design methods are in place, the engineers will have the criteria to judge the quality of the designs that they inspect. That is the time to introduce design inspections.

After successfully introducing the inspection program and the design courses, you will have a substantial level of credibility and a modest staff. Then, you can think about tackling a more challenging improvement effort. This would be a good time to get yourself or one of your people trained as a PSP instructor and TSP launch coach.[6] While this will take a few months and cost a little money, the training is readily available and will enable you to introduce the PSP and TSP into one or two projects in your organization.

After getting one or more staff members qualified as PSP instructors, look for a trial project. Training volunteers is the easy-sounding approach, but to successfully introduce the PSP and TSP, you must focus on entire teams, including the managers. Once you identify a team and have a qualified PSP instructor available, you can introduce the PSP and TSP in only three or four months. Even though it will generally be several months before you have data on completed projects, TSP's planning and tracking benefits will be apparent very quickly.

6. Watts S. Humphrey. 1995. *A Discipline for Software Engineering*. Reading, MA: Addison-Wesley.

To spread the PSP and TSP to other projects, first convince the managers. To convince the engineers to participate, get the first TSP team to meet with the potential new team, and have all the managers leave the room. The engineers from the first project will be most effective at convincing the second team to use the PSP and TSP. Once you have a few TSP teams in place, you will have the data, experience, and support to launch a broader-based improvement program.

Assuming that your tactically focused improvement efforts have so far been successful, you can start to move toward a broader-based CMM improvement effort. Be cautious about moving too fast and keep your proposals modest until you are reasonably certain that they will be accepted. The next step is to fix the organization's commitment system.

The commitment process defines the way organizations commit project costs and schedules to customers. Improvements in the commitment system generally produce significant benefits very quickly. The basic principles of the software commitment system are well known.[7] Improving the commitment system is an important early step in a CMM-based improvement program.

Changing the commitment system is much more difficult than anything you have attempted so far. For some reason, managers who make plans before they commit to constructing a building, starting a manufacturing program, or even taking a trip, do not appreciate the need for planning software projects.

---

7. See the following:

Watts S. Humphrey. 1989. *Managing the Software Process*. Reading, MA: Addison-Wesley.

Watts S. Humphrey. 2000. *Introduction to the Team Software Process*[SM]. Reading, MA: Addison-Wesley.

Mark C. Paulk and others. 1995. *The Capability Maturity Model: Guidelines for Improving the Software Process*. Reading, MA: Addison-Wesley.

Changing the commitment process requires that the managers change their behavior. If you thought changing engineering behavior was difficult, wait until you try to change management behavior. This is why a full-scale CMM-based process improvement program can be difficult to launch.

While the commitment system is probably the most important area to improve, unlike inspections or the PSP/TSP, it cannot be done for only one or two projects. If you can change the commitment system, however, you should be able to launch a full-scale, strategic-based process improvement program. This should include a full CMM-based effort, as well as an expansion of the PSP and TSP to cover all of the development and maintenance projects in the organization.

## 6.12 WHAT MANAGEMENT EXPECTS FROM A TEAM LEADER

As team leader, you are part of management. While this does not necessarily mean that you will have an office and an assistant or that you will control salaries or promotions, it does set you apart from the team members. The essential difference is that you are now expected to get work done by delegating to other people rather than doing it all yourself. Most new managers have trouble accepting the fact that their job is to lead the people who do the work, not to do the work themselves.

While most team leaders who have been developers see nothing wrong with actually doing much of the work themselves, this is rarely a good idea and it can even damage your ability to be an effective leader. Even if you are the most skilled designer on the team, your job is to lead the team, not to be the lead designer. While you may have to provide detailed guidance on the design work, the best leaders show their team members how to do their jobs but do not step in and do the work themselves.

On a small team, you may decide to take on some of the team's roles and tasks yourself. But that must never be your primary concern and it must not distract you from the principal job of leading, guiding, supporting, and protecting the team. As far as management is concerned, your job is to use all of the team's resources to do this job. Everything else is secondary.

Some other things management expects of you are as follows.

- You will get this job done on the schedule and with the resources you have been given.
- The products you produce will meet both the stated and the implied requirements.
- You will keep management posted on your team's progress.
- You will inform management of any problems or issues in time for them to take corrective action.
- You will work cooperatively with all of the other parts of the organization.
- You will abide by all of the organization's rules, regulations, and standards.

While management's expectations are not very surprising, what your team members expect is much less well defined and often contradictory. Initially, the team members will have a collection of individual expectations. While these expectations could vary widely, there are a few common ones that team members almost always have of their leaders.

First, like everyone else, creative people share a basic need for job security. They want to keep their jobs and are understandably concerned about management's views of their performance. However, professionals' views of what makes a job interesting and rewarding often differ somewhat from management's priorities.

Second, what often is surprising to management is that the top priority for most development professionals is not about the product or the schedule. It is to work on a cohesive and cooperative team. In fact, even when the result is a total business disaster, if the team provided a rewarding personal experience, the team members will view the project as a success.[8]

Third, the team members like to be successful. While this expectation will vary considerably from member to member, most would like to finish the job on time and to produce a successful product.

Fourth, and this expectation often ranks ahead of finishing the job on time, many team members want to do technical work that is interesting and that satisfies their personal goals and aspirations. This expectation is often hard to satisfy since it can change quickly. While a developer might be very interested in tackling a new challenge, once he or she has successfully handled a similar task once or twice, such challenges are much less appealing. In fact, every engineering challenge is much like a mystery story. Once you know the ending, it is easy to lose interest.

In many respects, management's priorities are very consistent with the team's basic interests. They want skilled and satisfied employees and they need a stable and reliable workforce. Where their interests differ, however, is on the importance of building a cohesive and rewarding team environment. While few managers would object to such an environment, they have not generally thought much about it or given it a very high priority.

Resolving these differing priorities is a key part of your job and it is what makes leading development work so interesting

---

8. Kurt R. Linberg. 1999. "Software Developer Perceptions about Software Project Failure: A Case Study." *The Journal of Systems and Software* 49, 177–192.

and rewarding. The reason is something that many team leaders do not appreciate until after they have led several projects: when teams are cohesive and cooperative, and when they find their work most rewarding and enjoyable, they also do the best work. And that is also when they are most likely to meet their committed schedules and to deliver quality products. Convincing management and the team of this fact will be one of your more interesting challenges.

Leadership is demanding, particularly for development work, but it is also exciting to have the support and allegiance of a capable, energetic, and enthusiastic team. You will find that once you have built a truly cohesive and energetic team, you will enjoy the work every bit as much as they do. However, to build such a team you must maintain a clear and consistent focus on the team's goals, set an example for the kind of performance you want, maintain high standards, and be responsible for all of the team's work.

## SOURCES

**6.1:** From *The Watts New Collection: Columns by the SEI's Watts Humphrey*, September 1998, "Your Date or Mine?"

**6.2:** From *TSP^SM: Leading a Development Team*, Chapter 9

**6.3:** From *PSP^SM: A Self-Improvement Process for Software Engineers*, Chapter 14

**6.4:** From *TSP^SM: Leading a Development Team*, Chapter 12

**6.5:** From *The Watts New Collection: Columns by the SEI's Watts Humphrey*, June 1998, "Why Does Software Work Take So Long?"

**6.6:** From *The Watts New Collection: Columns by the SEI's Watts Humphrey*, Second Quarter 2002, "Surviving Failure"

**6.7:** From *The Watts New Collection: Columns by the SEI's Watts Humphrey,* Number 5, 2007, "Being Your Own Boss—Part II: The Autocratic Manager"

**6.8:** From *The Watts New Collection: Columns by the SEI's Watts Humphrey,* Number 5, 2007, "Being Your Own Boss—Part II: The Autocratic Manager"

**6.9:** From *The Watts New Collection: Columns by the SEI's Watts Humphrey,* September 1999, "Getting Management Support for Process Improvement"

**6.10:** From *The Watts New Collection: Columns by the SEI's Watts Humphrey,* December 1999, "Making the Strategic Case for Process Improvement"

**6.11:** From *The Watts New Collection: Columns by the SEI's Watts Humphrey,* March 2000, "Making the Tactical Case for Process Improvement"

**6.12:** From *TSP^SM: Leading a Development Team,* Chapter 1

# PART IV
## Managing Yourself

# 7

# Taking Control of Your Work

**7.11 Manage Commitments So You Don't Forget Any or Run Out of Time**
Until you learn to manage your commitments, you will often face unpleasant consequences.

**7.12 What Do You Want From Life?**
Challenge yourself to do superior work, and you will be surprised at what you can accomplish.

**7.13 Devote Yourself to Excellence**
Treat every project as a way to build talent rather than merely treating your talent as a way to build projects.

## 7.1 A DEFINED PROCESS WILL HELP YOU IMPROVE

Process design and development is not all that hard if you approach it properly and if you have actually used such a process yourself. It is surprisingly easy and the results are truly amazing.

Take the example of Maurice Greene, who broke the world record for the 100-meter race in Athens on June 16, 1999. Although he had always been a fast runner, he had not been winning races and was becoming discouraged. Then he went to see coach John Smith in Los Angeles. Smith videotaped Greene doing a sprint, and then broke Greene's ten-second run into 11 phases. He analyzed each phase and showed Greene how to maximize his performance in every one. This became Greene's defined and measured personal running process. After several months of coaching, Greene started winning world records, and for several years he was known as the fastest man alive.

How would you like to be the fastest software developer alive, or the best by any other measure you choose? Today, we have no way to even talk about this subject. Our work is essentially unmeasured. Like Greene, we are all trying harder, but we don't know whether we are improving, or even what improvement would look like. That is what a defined, measured, planned, and quality-controlled personal process can do for you. Although you may not want to put in the months of rigorous training needed to become a world champion, we all want to do our jobs in the best way we can. With a defined and measured process, not only will you know how well you are doing your job today, you will see how to improve, and to keep improving as long as you keep developing software.

## 7.2 BE YOUR OWN BOSS, AND DON'T BE A VICTIM

When I ask software developers about the issues they face and the problems that typically cause their projects to fail, I hear lots of complaints. There are many reasons why our projects fail, and we typically blame somebody else for the failures. Management gave us an impossible schedule, the customer changed the requirements, the organization has an impossible bureaucracy, or there are too many meetings and distractions. This is victim talk. Have you ever heard a first-class surgeon, a top-flight scientist, or a winning ballplayer talk like this?

Winners win; they don't complain. It is the perpetual losers who complain about how unfair life is and how somebody else is always to blame for their failures. While it is true that software development is a challenging business and that we almost always face tight schedules and changing requirements, these problems can be managed. However, they can be managed only if you know how to manage them.

You might wonder why more software professionals don't manage themselves, and why essentially all software developers act like victims. These smart and capable people seem willing to spend their lives behaving like losers. The principal reason is that nobody ever showed them how to break out of their victim trap. The second and almost as important reason is that, even though self-management methods are not that difficult, they are not obvious.

The alternative to being a victim is to take charge. There are two parts to doing this. The first is the hard part: actually taking control of your own work. Then, once you know how to manage yourself, the second part is much easier: convincing management to let you manage yourself.

## 7.3 HOW TO IMPROVE THE QUALITY OF YOUR WORK

When I was in the U.S. Navy, I had to learn to shoot a machine gun. Training started with shotguns and clay pigeons. My scores were terrible and they didn't improve, even with practice. After watching me for a while, the instructor suggested that I try shooting left-handed. Being right-handed, I found this unnatural at first, but after a few trial shots, I consistently got near-perfect scores.

There are several parts to this example. First, measurements are needed to diagnose a problem. By knowing how many clay pigeons I hit and missed, the instructor and I could easily see that I had to do something differently. Next, we had to use these measurements in some kind of objective analysis. By watching me, the instructor could analyze the process I used to shoot the shotgun—the steps I followed in loading, positioning, tracking, aiming, and firing the gun. The instructor's objective was to discover which steps were the source of my problem. He quickly zeroed in on aim and suggested that I make a change.

Finally, and most important, came the change itself. Process improvement is difficult because people are reluctant to try new things. Their current habits seem so natural they can't believe the change would help. I had always been right-handed and it never occurred to me to shoot with the left. Once I made the suggested change, however, my scores improved.

Defining measures is not always easy, but it is almost always possible. Once you have defined measures for your work, you must gather and analyze data. If you need to improve, you next analyze the process to see where to make changes. Finally, to improve, you must actually change what you do.

If I hadn't changed my process, I could have kept score for years without becoming a better shot. Measuring alone will not produce improvement, and neither will trying harder. How you work largely determines the results you get. If you continue working the same old way, you will continue producing the same old results.

The steps needed to change the way you work are the same as the steps I followed in learning to shoot clay pigeons. They are not complicated.

- **Define the quality goal.** Obviously, my objective was to hit the target as often as I could, 100 percent being the ultimate goal.

- **Measure product quality.** The instructor and I could see that my scores were terrible and that something had to be done.

- **Understand the process.** The instructor observed what I did to see what I should change.

- **Adjust the process.** He suggested that I shoot left-handed.

- **Use the adjusted process.** I next shot several more rounds, but this time I shot left-handed.

- **Measure the results.** We counted the number of pigeons I hit and missed.

- **Compare the results with the goal.** From these data, we could see that my scores were dramatically better.

- **Recycle and continue improving.** Because learning to shoot clay pigeons was simple, continuous process improvement was not needed.

With more complex processes, several cycles are generally required. With a sophisticated process like software development, the improvement cycles should never end.

## 7.4 THE 18-HOUR WORK WEEK

Have you ever started what you thought was a two- or three-day job and have it stretch into a week or two? Before deciding you are just bad at estimating, look at how you spent your time. You will find you spend much less time on projects than you imagine. For example, on one project, several engineers used time logs to track their time in minutes. They averaged only 16 to 18 hours a week on project tasks. They were surprised because they all worked a standard 40-hour week.

This information soon turned out to be helpful. They were on a critical project and were falling behind. When they looked at the data, they found the design work took 50 percent longer than estimated. They knew they had a choice: either do the tasks faster, or put in more time. While there was pressure to race through the design, skip inspections, and rush into coding, the team resisted. They knew this would probably result in many errors and a lot of test time.

To meet their schedule, they needed to average 30 task hours a week. They all tried valiantly to do this, but they realized that just trying harder would not work. They went on overtime and started early in the morning, worked late some evenings, or came in on weekends. While they averaged 30 task hours a week, they had to work more than 50 hours a week to do it. They also got back on schedule.

Because this team had detailed time information, they could recognize and address their problem in time to save the project. The data identified the problem and pointed them toward the solution. Without good data on where your time goes, your estimates will always be inaccurate and you won't know how to improve.

When people say they are working harder, they actually mean they are working longer hours. Barring major technology changes, the time it takes to do most tasks is relatively stable. The real variable is the time you spend on the tasks. But to manage the time you spend, you have to track it, and practically nobody does. Consider the following:

- Our lives are filled with interruptions.

- Software people do many kinds of tasks, and only some contribute directly to our projects.

- Our processes are often informal and our working practices ad hoc.

- Even if we wanted to, it is hard to do demanding intellectual work for long uninterrupted periods.

One engineer told me she had recently started to track her time and found she was spending much more time on interruptions than on her real work. For example, on one task of 108 minutes, her interruption time was over 300 minutes. This lost time, however, was not in big hour-long blocks but from an incessant stream of little 5- and 10-minute interruptions.

Interruptions come from many sources:

- Telephone calls

- Other engineers asking for help

- A coffee or rest break

- Supply problems (i.e., printer or copier out of paper)

- Equipment problems (the network dies)

- A power failure or a snow storm (everybody leaves)

Every interruption breaks your train of thought and takes time away from your work. With unplanned interruptions, you lose your place in the work and, when the interruption is over, you have to reconstruct where you were. This also causes errors.

For example, when I am in the middle of a design, I am often working on several things at the same time. While thinking through some logical structure, I realize that a name is misleading, a type must be changed, or an interface is incomplete. If I am interrupted in the middle of this, I often have trouble remembering all these details. While I have been unable to control the interruptions, I have found that maintaining an issue log helps me remember what I was working on when interrupted.

Interruptions are a fact of life, but there are many ways to deal with them. Use "DO NOT DISTURB" signs and establish an ethic where everybody (even the managers) respects them. Forward phone calls or even unplug or turn off the phone. Also consider getting permission to work at home for a day or two a week.

Another way to manage interruptions is to get in the habit of using an issue-tracking log. Then, when you think of something you need to do, make a note of it in the log so you will remember to do it later and you won't forget it when the phone rings. While you will still have to handle these issues, you are less likely to forget them and you can do them at a planned time.

Also, use this same principle with interruptions. When someone calls in the middle of a design problem, tell them you'll get back and then make a note on a sticky so you don't forget.

Most engineers also spend a lot of time on non-engineering tasks. Examples are

- Handling mail
- Setting up or updating their computing systems

- Going to meetings
- Looking for some specification, process, standard, or manual
- Assisting other engineers
- Attending classes

Few software development groups have adequate support. No one sets up or maintains his or her development system, few have groups to handle product packaging and release, and there is no clerical or secretarial support for mail, phone, or expense accounts. What is more, even when they have such support, many engineers don't know how to use it. This means that most of us spend more time on clerical and support work than on our principal development tasks. And every hour spent on these tasks is an hour we can't spend on development.

Finally, creative development is hard work. When designing a product or a system, we need uninterrupted time. But we cannot design complex products for more than a few hours at a time. The same is true of testing, reviewing, inspecting, coding, compiling, and many other tasks.

One laboratory decided to set up a dedicated group of experts to inspect a large and important product in final test. Every module that had test problems was sent to this group. For a while, they cleaned up a lot of defect-prone modules. Then, one of them later told me, they could no longer see the code they were inspecting. Everything began to blur. They even saw source code in their sleep.

Designing, coding, reviewing, inspecting, and testing are intensely difficult tasks. To have any hope of producing quality products, we must occasionally take breaks. But, to be reasonably efficient, and to do high-quality work, we need to control our own breaks, not take them when the phone rings or when somebody barges into our office or cubicle. Studies show that when engineers spend all their time on their principal jobs, their performance deteriorates. Some reasonable percentage of time on other tasks such as planning, process improvement, quality analysis, or writing papers can improve engineering performance. You will get more and better work done in the remaining 75 percent of your time than you would have accomplished in 100 percent of dedicated time.[1]

To manage your personal work, you need to know where your time goes. This means you need to track your time. This is not hard, but it does require discipline. I suggest you get in the habit of using a time recording log. When doing so, enter the tasks and the times when you start and stop these tasks, and also keep track of interruption times. If you do this, you will soon see where your time goes. Then you can figure out what to do about it.

## 7.5 FIGHT PHANTOM ISSUES IN HIGH-PRESSURE PROJECTS

When software projects fail, it is generally because of teamwork problems and not technical issues. DeMarco says that

> The success or failure of a project is seldom due to technical issues. You almost never find yourself asking "has the state of the art advanced far enough so that this program can be written?" Of course it has. If the project does go down the tubes, it will be non-technical, human interaction problems that do it in. The team will fail to bind, or the developers will fail to gain rapport

---

1. For a brief discussion of this issue, see Watts S. Humphrey. 1997. *Managing Technical People: Innovation, Teamwork, and the Software Process.* Reading, MA: Addison-Wesley. A more complete discussion is in Donald C. Pelz and Frank M. Andrews. 1966. *Scientists in Organizations: Productive Climates for Research and Development.* New York: John Wiley & Sons, 56, 65.

with the users, or people will fight interminably over meaningless methodological issues.[2]

One significant "people" problem is the inability of software teams to handle pressure, especially the pressure to meet an aggressive development schedule. Often, teams respond to this pressure by taking shortcuts, using poor methods, or gambling on a new (to them) language, tool, or technique.

Excessive pressure can be destructive. It causes people to worry and to imagine problems and difficulties that may not be real. Rather than help you to cope in an orderly and constructive way, pressure causes worry about many unknown (and often phantom) issues. And sometimes pressure can cause you to act as if the phantom issues were real. This behavior can have untold consequences for your project, your organization, and even your self-esteem.

When your team knows how to handle the pressure of a tight schedule, you can feel the difference. Before starting a job, you generally don't know precisely what is involved. But after you make a plan and get started, you feel relieved. This is true even if the job is larger than you thought. The reason you feel relieved is that you are now dealing with a known problem rather than an unknown worry.

Pressure is something that you feel. For example, you may need to do a task whether or not you think you can do it. The greater the need and the more doubt you have about your ability to do the task, the greater the pressure. Because pressure is internally generated, you have the power to manage it yourself, but first you must find the source of the pressure and then figure

---

2. Tom DeMarco. 1988. "Looking for Lost Keys." *Software Magazine*, April 1988, 2.

out how to deal with it. The apparent source of pressure in software projects is the need to meet a tight schedule. This schedule could come from management, your instructor, or your peers.

The real source of pressure, however, is ourselves. It comes from our natural desire to accomplish what our managers, instructors, or peers want. When this pressure is coupled with normal self-doubts about our ability to perform, it can become destructive. This is particularly true for new software teams that have not yet learned how to handle the normal challenges of their projects. Teams need to know how to work efficiently and to produce quality products, especially when they are under intense schedule pressure.

By guiding teams through a strategy and planning process, the Team Software Process (TSP) shows teams how to handle pressure. They analyze the job, devise a strategy for doing the work, estimate the sizes of the products they will build, and then make a plan. Because unrealistic schedules are the principal cause of software project problems, the TSP helps teams manage their projects more effectively. When they are able to manage their work, teams are much more likely to do a quality job.

## 7.6 SUPPORT STAFF CAN HELP YOU

Learn how to use support. While few engineers have a support staff to help them, many who do don't know how to use them. If you have a support person, think about every clerical-type task before you do it. Can this person do it for you? Even though it may take longer at first, use them whenever you can. At first the result may need to be redone. But be patient and help the support people understand your problems with their work. It will pay off in the long run.

Perhaps most important, learn to plan. Plan your own work and urge your teammates and the project leader to start planning.

Proper planning takes time, but it can save much more time than it costs. You will end up planning anyway, but it is much better to do it in an orderly way, and not at the coffee machine.

When planning, remember that you can do demanding work only for so long. I lose my ability to do intense creative work after an hour and a half to two hours. I need to stop for a break or even to switch to some other kind of work. Further, during these intense sessions, frequent short interruptions offer no relief. It then takes an extra effort to reconstruct my thought process.

What I suggest is to intersperse various kinds of work throughout your day. Do creative work when you are most fresh and productive and then switch to your email or an administrative task. Then perhaps do a design or code review possibly followed by a process-improvement task or data analysis. By varying the task types, your creative work will be of higher quality and you will actually get more done.

When you regularly make plans, a defined process will save a lot of time. The process provides a framework for gathering historical data and a template for making plans. And, by using historical data, your estimates will be more accurate.

Finally, if you don't have administrative or technical support, use your time log to see what this lack costs you. Then tell your managers and show them your data. It might help them see the cost advantages of adequately supporting their engineers. Remember that the amount of work you produce is principally determined by two things:

1. The time the tasks will take
2. How much time you have available for these tasks

To manage your work, you must know where your time goes. Only then can you judge how much work you can do and when you will finish it.

## 7.7 THE LOGIC OF TIME MANAGEMENT

The logical basis for time management is as follows.

*You will likely spend your time this week much the way you spent time last week.* In general, the way you spent your time last week provides a fair approximation of the way you will spend time in future weeks. There are, however, many exceptions. During exam week, for example, you may not attend the same classes and you will probably spend more time studying and less time doing homework.

*To make realistic plans, you have to track the way you spend time.* While you may think you know how you spent time last week, you would probably be surprised by actual data. People remember some things and forget others. For example, the time spent doing homework is probably much less than estimated, while the time at meals or relaxing with friends is often much more than expected. Our memories tend to minimize the time we spend on things that seem to move quickly because we enjoy doing them. Conversely, slow-paced, boring, or difficult activities seem to take much longer than the reality. Therefore, to know where your time goes, you need to keep an accurate record.

To check the accuracy of your time estimates and plans, you must document them and later compare them with what you actually do. While this will not be a serious problem in school, it is critically important for working engineers. Planning is a skill that few people have mastered. There are, however, known planning methods that can be learned and practiced. The first step in learning to make good plans is to make plans. Then write down your plan so you will later have something to compare with your actual data.

*To make more accurate plans, determine where your previous plans were in error and what you could have done better.* When you do the planned job, record the time you spend. These time data will be most useful if noted in some detail. For example, when doing course work, separately record the time you spend attending class, reading the textbook, writing programs, and studying for exams. When writing larger programs, you will similarly find it helpful to record the time for various parts of the job—designing the program, writing code, compiling, and testing. While this level of detail is not needed for very short tasks, it can be helpful when working on projects that take several hours or more.

When you have a documented copy of your plan and have recorded the actual time you spent, you can easily compare the actual results with the original plan. You will then see where the plan was in error and how your planning process can be improved. The key to accurate planning is to consistently make plans and compare them each time with subsequent actual results. You will then see how to make better plans.

*To manage your time, plan your time and then follow the plan.* Figuring out what you could do to produce better plans is the easy part. Actually doing it is far more difficult. The world is full of resolutions that are never fulfilled, like sticking with a diet or quitting smoking.

Initially, following a plan is likely to be difficult. While there are many possible reasons, the most common is that the plan was not very good. Until you try to follow it, you probably will not know that. By working to the plan, you gain the first of two benefits: You learn where the plan was in error, which will help you better plan the next project.

The second benefit of working to the plan is that you will do the job the way you planned to. While this may not seem terribly important, it is. Many of the problems in software engineering are caused by ill-considered shortcuts, carelessness, and inattention to detail. In most cases, the proper methods were known and specified but just not followed. Learning to establish usable plans is thus important, but learning to follow these plans is absolutely crucial.

Another and more subtle benefit of working to a plan is that it actually changes your behavior. With a plan, you are less likely to waste time deciding what to do next. The plan also helps you focus on what you are doing. You are less likely to be distracted and more likely to be efficient.

To practice time management, the first step is to understand how you now spend time. This calls for several steps:

*Categorize your major activities.* When you start tracking time, you will probably find that most of the time is spent on relatively few activities. This is normal. To accomplish anything, we must focus on the few things that are most important. If you break your time into too many categories, it will be hard to make sense of the data. Three to five categories should be enough for tracking time for one course. If you later need more detail, break the more general categories into subcategories.

*Record the time spent on each major activity.* It takes a fair amount of personal discipline to consistently record time. To keep an accurate record, record the time at the start and end of every major work category. At first you will often forget to do this, but after some practice, it will become second nature.

*Record time in a standard way.* Standardizing your time log is necessary because the volume of time data will grow very quickly. If you don't record and carefully store these data, they will get lost or disorganized. Messy or confused data are also hard to find or interpret. If you don't intend to handle the data properly, you might as well not gather the data at all.

*Keep the time data in a convenient place.* Because you will need to keep the time recording log with you, keep it in a convenient place. This is one of the principal uses for the engineering notebook.

## 7.8 BEING RESPONSIBLE IS ABOUT OWNERSHIP AND ATTITUDE

By being responsible, I am talking about ownership and attitude. Are you responsible for your own behavior? Are you willing to step up to and address issues when you see problems? Behaving this way is rarely easy, as Judy, a lead software engineer, discovered in the following example.

Some years ago, when I reviewed a small software project, the schedule problem was not yet obvious to anyone except the development team. This was July, and Judy, the team leader, knew that the year-end deadline was impossible. She did not want to tell her manager, however, because she had complained about the schedule at the beginning of the project and had been ignored. So she and the team kept plugging away, hoping for some miracle to save them. There was no miracle, however, and the project was late, management was irate, and Judy and her small team were considered failures.

Judy's project was to modify an accounting program so that it would conform to a new tax law. The work had to be done by the end of the year, because that was when the new law took effect. Judy and two other engineers had been working for several months, and they knew that the planned date was impossible. They also knew, however, that there was no choice, for this was the law. So she blamed Congress and her management for the problem.

Sound familiar? This is a little like blaming your problems on the weather or a bad astrological sign. There was no point in trying to change the law. Judy knew that she could not. The problem was that no one—not Judy, not her manager, not the managers above him—acted responsibly. In the last analysis, however, Judy was the only person who really understood the problem. The other two engineers were totally engrossed in the project details, and the managers kept hoping that things would work out. To behave responsibly, Judy should have convinced her manager that the schedule truly was impossible, at least for the three engineers assigned to the job. Although that would not have been easy to do, it was the only responsible course of action.

Being responsible is a way to look at life. When faced with a problem, we generally have three choices.

1. We can get emotional, cry, wave our arms, or blame other people.

2. We can ignore the problem and keep grinding ahead in the hope that things will somehow work out.

3. We can step up to the challenge, look around for what we can constructively do, and then work to get it done.

Being responsible means taking choice 3. We must either control the circumstances of our lives, or these circumstances will control us. To see what I mean, consider another example.

On Friday afternoon, an engineer in a software company's New York City laboratory learned that he had to be in California for an important Monday morning meeting. When he went to the laboratory cashier's office for a travel advance, however, he found that it had closed early, and the cashier was at a finance department meeting. The engineer tried to get the meeting interrupted so that he could get the money, but the finance manager's secretary would not interrupt the meeting.

At this point, the engineer had a choice: Would he be a victim of this situation, or would he act responsibly? He could have just given up and said that he couldn't make it to the Monday meeting, but he saw the problem as a challenge.

So he went to his boss and told him the problem. The boss also called the finance manager. Again the secretary refused to interrupt the meeting. The manager also refused to give up, however, so they both went to the laboratory director. The director called the secretary and told her to have the finance manager call him immediately. The finance manager did call, and the problem was quickly resolved.

Although this might seem like a minor problem, the world is full of minor problems, and any one of these problems can delay things, cause inconvenience, or even result in serious problems. Often, no one has been given responsibility for addressing any of these problems. And if no one decides to handle them, they will fester, and some will continue to cause problems, possibly for years.

It is uniquely human to take charge, to address problems, and to seek to change the world. So what does being responsible involve, and why is it hard? Take Judy's case. When I looked at her project in early July, the three engineers had been working for several months and it was obvious to them that they were not going to finish on time.

Of course, the source of the problem was that Judy's manager had been unreasonable at the very beginning of the project. Rather than have Judy and her two engineers make a plan that they felt was achievable, he demanded an impossible schedule. He also, it turns out, faced the same unreasonable demands from his management. The point is that with an impossible schedule, the project will be late, regardless of the law. The responsible actions for Judy and her managers would have been to understand and address the problem at the beginning, and not just blindly proceed in the hope that things would somehow work out.

In addition to unreasonable management, Judy and her team had another problem: she had only stated an opinion that the schedule was too tight. As long as it was a question of opinions, her manager preferred his opinion to hers. However, if she had made a detailed plan, she might have convinced him of the problem. Then he could have taken action. He might have added staff in an attempt to meet the schedule, or he could have alerted the users to prepare backup procedures. But doing nothing was irresponsible. In the end, everyone lost.

## 7.9 DELAY IS ALMOST ALWAYS THE WORST ALTERNATIVE

Why is it difficult to act responsibly? Actually, it is not difficult at all; people just think it is. The reason is that most of us are afraid that we won't be listened to, or we are unsure of our responsibilities. When we are unsure, we hang back to see whether someone else will handle the problem. Usually, however, no one else has clear responsibility either, so the problem just festers. In Judy's case, Congress had set the date and her manager had agreed to the project. So he was responsible and not Judy. Although it sounds rational to put blame where it belongs, doing so invariably leads to failed projects. Acting responsibly can seem risky. In fact, it is the least risky alternative.

When a project appears to the engineers to be in trouble, it almost certainly is. When people keep quiet and hope someone else will recognize the problem, the issue gets progressively harder to address. Every day that you wait to act is a day that you can't use to solve the problem. Delay also exposes you to the question of why you delayed telling management. If you can say that you just found out about the problem, that is reasonable. But if you have to admit that you have known for months but lacked the nerve to tell someone, you are more likely to be criticized. So delay is almost always the worst alternative.

Speaking up involves exposing yourself to criticism. Responsible actions often involve changing the status quo, and this never looks easy, particularly if you are an engineer and the status quo was established by a senior manager. But when the facts are known and senior managers understand the facts, they are usually reasonable.

Of course, what makes stating the facts risky is the chance that the senior manager will be unreasonable. Because engineers rarely know these managers and because these engineers will rarely be blamed for not personally taking action, it seems much safer to wait and see whether someone else will solve the problem. Although that is always an option, it is irresponsible.

Perhaps the best example of how facts can change an executive's point of view was cited by Covey in his wonderful book, *The 7 Habits of Highly Effective People.*[3]

> Two battleships assigned to the training squadron had been at sea on maneuvers in heavy weather for several days. I was serving on the lead battleship and was on watch on the bridge as night fell. The visibility was poor with patchy fog, so the captain remained on the bridge keeping an eye on all activities.
>
> Shortly after dark, the lookout on the wing of the bridge reported, "Light, bearing on the starboard bow."
>
> "Is it steady or moving astern?" the captain called out.
>
> Lookout replied, "Steady, captain," which meant we were on a dangerous collision course with that ship.
>
> The captain then called to the signalman, "Signal that ship: We are on a collision course, advise you change course 20 degrees."
>
> Back came a signal, "Advisable for you to change course 20 degrees."
>
> The captain said, "Send, I'm a captain, change course 20 degrees."

3. Stephen R. Covey. 1990. *The 7 Habits of Highly Effective People: Powerful Lessons in Personal Change*. New York: Simon & Schuster, 33.

"I'm a seaman second class," came the reply. "You had better change course 20 degrees."

By that time, the captain was furious. He spat out, "Send, I'm a battleship. Change course 20 degrees."

Back came a flashing light, "I'm a lighthouse."

We changed course.

So if you know the facts and can make these facts clear to management, think of yourself as a lighthouse. Then all these executive battleships will have to pay attention.

## 7.10 BEING COMMITTED IS A STATE OF MIND

Being committed is a state of mind. For whatever reason, you have undertaken to do something, and you feel you should do it. A commitment, however, is more than just something you intend to do; there is also someone who expects you to do it. This, in fact, is the key issue with commitments: Who is the person to whom you are committed? In the legal or contractual sense, you are committed to someone else: your professor, your manager, your employer. More important, however, are the deeper commitments you make to yourself.

The principal problem with many software schedules and plans is that management views them as contract-like commitments, but the software engineers do not view them as personal commitments. The difference, as we shall see, is largely in how the commitments are made.

With a contractual commitment, two or more people must agree on the intended action before it is a commitment. For example, Mr. A and Ms. B agree that Mr. A will provide some product or do some task for Ms. B. An example is your commitment to your teacher to do a homework assignment for a course.

Another example would be your agreement to write a program for a customer.

When Mr. A makes a commitment, he agrees with Ms. B to perform a specified task by some defined time and for some reward or compensation. This points out two more elements of commitments. In addition to agreeing on the task, the parties also agreed on the time it is to be done and on the payment or other consideration Mr. A will receive in return. Again, an example would be your agreement to complete and submit homework in one week and the instructor's agreement to give you a grade on the work. Another example could be a customer's obligation to pay you for developing and installing some software.

A key characteristic of personal commitments is that they are voluntary. Suppose, for example, that your customer finds he needs the program sooner and tells you to finish it two weeks earlier than originally agreed. He never asked if you could finish by this earlier date, and you did not agree. You were just told the new deadline. Even though you may try to meet the new date, you probably won't feel personally committed to doing so.

To become truly committed, you must have thoughtfully considered the alternatives and decided that this is something you can and will do. Being told by someone that you must do it will not make you personally committed. In fact, when people are ordered to do things, they often feel threatened and angry. They resent the person making the directive and may even want to retaliate. One way to retaliate, of course, would be to not do the demanded action. While such a reaction to a normal business request may seem childish, many people unconsciously respond this way.

True agreement is the most important single characteristic of a personal commitment. The parties must agree on what is to be done, when it will be completed, and what will be given in return. A true commitment is both personal and contractual and it requires an explicit and voluntary agreement between two or more parties on

- What will be done
- The criteria for determining that it is done
- Who will do it
- When it will be done
- The compensation or other consideration to be given in return
- Who will provide this compensation or consideration

In addition to the characteristics already described, commitments should be responsibly made and properly managed. You can make sure your commitments are responsible and well managed as follows.

*Analyze the job before agreeing to the commitment.* Both parties must enter into the commitment in good faith. You are personally committed and really intend to do the job and the other party intends to provide suitable compensation in return.

The question, however, is the degree to which you have both made sure you can meet the commitment. For example, have you examined the job in sufficient detail to know you can do it? Similarly, does the other party have the capability to compensate you? Too often, software commitments are based on little more than hope. Even when both parties truly intend to perform, mere good intentions do not provide a reasonable basis for a sound commitment.

*Support the commitment with a plan.* For a job of any size, the way to responsibly make a commitment is to first make a plan for the work. Planning does involve some effort, but it need not take very long. In fact, if you have had experience in making formal plans, you can usually complete them quite quickly.

*Document the agreement.* While this may seem obvious, it is not. There is a common misperception that honest people should need only a few words and a handshake. But words are often misunderstood. Even after two people orally agree, they often have trouble agreeing on a written statement of the agreement.

This means that their original agreement was superficial and not real. The second problem concerns what the two parties will do in the event of problems. That, in fact, is the principal reason for most written contracts. You do not need a contract when everything goes according to plan—you need one if there are problems.

*If unable to meet the commitment, promptly tell the other party and try to minimize the impact on that person.* When you have learned to manage your commitments, you will almost always meet them. Unfortunately, even with the best plans, the job will occasionally be more complex than you expected or something unforeseen may come up.

## 7.11 MANAGE COMMITMENTS SO YOU DON'T FORGET ANY OR RUN OUT OF TIME

The principal reason to manage your commitments is so you don't overlook or forget any. Working engineers have many commitments. They participate in reviews, write reports, attend meetings, make program corrections, and submit updates to program modules. They may have to document designs, answer customer calls, meet vendors, or participate on committees. It is not unusual for working engineers to juggle a dozen commitments simultaneously. It is thus important to learn how to manage commitments so you do not drop or forget any of them.

Another reason for managing your commitments is to help you when the work you need to do exceeds the time available. If you plan your work, you shouldn't run out of time too often, but it can be an occasional problem even when you make commitments responsibly. In this situation, quickly identify those commitments that are exposed and promptly notify the other parties.

Until you learn to manage your commitments, you will often face some of the following unpleasant consequences:

*Work required exceeds time available.* You will frequently have more to do than you can accomplish. If you do not keep a list of your commitments, you may take on new commitments when you should not. You might, for example, make a social engagement when you had a homework assignment due the next day. Late in the evening you remember the assignment and then have to stay up all night to get it done. Worse yet, you might not remember it at all.

*Failure to meet commitments.* Software development jobs are often more complex than expected. When you do not have an orderly way of making commitments, you are likely to assume the job is simpler than it really is. You will then be overcommitted from the moment you start working on the job.

*Misplaced priorities.* When overcommitted, people often set priorities based on what must be done first rather than what is most important. When there is more to do than you can possibly handle, it is natural to work on the next thing that must be done. Unfortunately, handling the immediate threat is often the wrong strategy.

When you are seriously overcommitted, you need to restructure all your commitments to fit what you can do. By deferring or dropping some of the immediate tasks, you may be able to meet the more important jobs that come later.

*Poor quality work.* Under schedule pressure, software engineers often feel pressed to cut corners. This is when careless or silly mistakes are more likely and when attention to quality is most needed. When time is short, engineers should take special care to avoid mistakes. Unfortunately, experience shows that this is the very circumstance when engineers and their managers are least likely to allow the time to do reviews, inspections, or thorough testing.

*Loss of trust.* If you frequently miss commitments, people will notice. They will learn that when you commit to something, you often don't keep to your word. Such a reputation is hard to repair and will affect your grades, your job ratings, your pay, and even your job security.

*Loss of respect for your judgment.* When people do not trust what you say, they are unlikely to ask for your opinion and they are more likely to insist that you work to unreasonable schedules.

The most important single asset a software engineer can have is a reputation for meeting commitments. For people to trust your word, you need to say what you plan to do and then do what you say.

## 7.12 WHAT DO YOU WANT FROM LIFE?

What do you want from your life? This is a big question that many people have trouble answering. A few points are worth considering as you think about the answer.

One way to get satisfaction from a job is to have status or power. People can get this by being a boss or being put in charge of an important service. Power and status can also be indirect, like making a lot of money, working for an important company, or driving a fancy car. These are all parts of "being" someone.

While there is nothing wrong with status, it is temporary. You may hold an important job for a while but, sooner or later, your next step will be down. Losing status can be a crisis. Some people are devastated when they first lose an important job. It is easy to confuse the importance of a job with personal importance.

I have known managers who were crushed by a demotion. They had built an image of themselves as important people. As long as they held a big job, everybody treated them as important. The minute they lost that job, however, they were just like everyone else. Nobody cared what they said and they stopped getting special treatment. They had lost the corner office and no longer had a secretary. This can be such a severe shock that some people have nervous breakdowns, heart attacks, or family crises. Their reward was status and it is gone.

The need is to decide what it is that you want. Think ahead. When you ultimately retire, what would a satisfying life look like? I suggest that what you have done will be far more rewarding than what you have been. If, for example, you plan to do engineering work, you probably have the instincts of a builder. Maybe you will build systems or components. You could end up building methods or processes. Or you might have a scientific bent and build theories or do research to build fundamental knowledge.

Whatever you build, however, quality will be key. You will get little satisfaction from sloppy work. Somehow, even if no one else finds out, you will know you did a sloppy job. This will destroy your pride in the work and it will limit your satisfaction with life. You cannot honestly say to yourself that you really believe in quality, but you will just get by this one time. There are always lots of excuses. You might even satisfy others with an expedient answer, but you will never satisfy yourself.

When you do quality work, you will be proud. Even if no one else knows, you know you did a first-class job and you are satisfied that you did your best. The surprising thing is that quality work gets known. It may take a long time, but sooner or later quality work is recognized. Whether you know it, you will get credit for the quality of your work.

So ask yourself this question: "Do I want to feel proud of what I do?" Most people would answer yes. But if you really mean it, you need to set personal standards and strive to meet them. When you meet these standards, raise them and strive again. Challenge yourself to do superior work and you will be surprised at what you can accomplish.

## 7.13 DEVOTE YOURSELF TO EXCELLENCE

As you look to the future, you will face many questions. How will your field evolve, and what can you do to meet the mounting challenges? While no one can know, your progress probably will be limited by your ability to build your personal skills. Make practice a part of every project and measure and observe your own work. You cannot stand still, so you should treat every project as a way to build talent rather than merely treating your talent as a way to build projects.

Deciding what you want from your chosen field is like asking what you want from life. Surprisingly often, people achieve their objectives, but in ways they did not expect. Life rarely turns out the way we plan. While our carefully developed strategies may go down in flames, a new and more rewarding opportunity shows up in the ashes. The key is to keep an open mind and to keep looking. In life, we all reach the same end, so we need to concentrate on the trip. Just as with a process, once you decide how you want to live, the rest will follow. Devote yourself to excellence, and you just might achieve it. That would be worth the trip.

## SOURCES

**7.1:** From *PSP*[SM]*: A Self-Improvement Process for Software Engineers,* Chapter 1

**7.2:** From *The Watts New Collection: Columns by the SEI's Watts Humphrey,* Number 8 2007, "Being Your Own Boss—Part IV: Being a Victim"

**7.3:** From *Introduction to the Personal Software Process*[SM]*,* Chapter 1

**7.4:** From *The Watts New Collection: Columns by the SEI's Watts Humphrey,* June 1998, "Why Does Software Work Take So Long?"

**7.5:** From *Introduction to the Team Software Process*[SM], Chapter 2

**7.6:** From *The Watts New Collection: Columns by the SEI's Watts Humphrey,* June 1998, "Why Does Software Work Take So Long?"

**7.7:** From *Introduction to the Personal Software Process*[SM], Chapter 2

**7.8:** From *Introduction to the Team Software Process*[SM], Chapter 16

**7.9:** From *Introduction to the Team Software Process*[SM], Chapter 16

**7.10:** From *Introduction to the Personal Software Process*[SM], Chapter 8

**7.11:** From *Introduction to the Personal Software Process*[SM], Chapter 8

**7.12:** From *Introduction to the Personal Software Process*[SM], Chapter 20

**7.13**: From *A Discipline for Software Engineering,* Chapter 14

# 8

# Learning to Lead

## 8.1 HOW YOU BEHAVE AFFECTS YOUR TEAM

The way you act, your feelings, and even your private opinions will influence your team. For example, if you doubt that your

213

team can succeed in its mission, even if you say nothing about your concerns, this belief will subtly affect your behavior. Your team will probably detect your doubts. When your team members sense that you do not believe in them, they will almost certainly fail.

If you do not believe that the team can succeed, sit down with the entire team and discuss your concerns. Don't tell them that you believe they will fail, but do get the risks and issues on the table and see if others share your concerns. Then, work with the team to figure out what must be done to succeed. Next, work with the team to make the required changes.

Your role is to motivate the team to do its utmost. To accomplish this, you must have confidence in all the members, believe that they can overcome the obstacles ahead, and trust that they are capable of producing extraordinary results. The most successful teams have energetic, enthusiastic, confident, and hard-driving leaders. If you don't have the required energy and drive, figure out what to change so that you do. If you can't see how to do that, either your team has a hopeless job or it needs a new leader.

Finally, you are the boss. Your job is to get this project done and to use the resources that you have been given to do it. However, as boss, you are responsible for everything that the team does. You will get credit for the developers' achievements and successes, but you will also be blamed for their mistakes and failures. In short, as far as management is concerned, you *are* the team. This means that you had better make sure that the job is done correctly.

If the team is going down a blind alley, is wasting time on unproductive tasks, or is doing poor quality work, you must sooner or later answer for the consequences. Therefore, you had better make sure that the work is done properly. Doing this in a way that builds and sustains team motivation is not easy and there is no simple prescription that will fit all situations. However, there are some principles that can help you to define your own prescriptions.

## 8.2 LEADERS SET AN EXAMPLE FOR THEIR TEAMS

To use a sports analogy, athletic teams strive to win every game. This typically means scoring more points than the opposition. Every team member knows what the goal is and strives both to score points and to prevent the opposition from scoring. While many strategies contribute to successful games, the goal is always clear, and it is the focus for everything that the team does.

In development work, goals are equally important, but they are rarely as clear. While the ultimate goal is usually understood by all, there is often considerable confusion about short-term goals. A significant part of your leadership job is to keep the team's goals clear and well defined and to ensure that every team member knows how his or her current tasks contribute to meeting that goal. In addition, you want all team members to work energetically to meet their goals. As each goal is met, you help the team to move on to the next immediate goals, continuing until you meet the final objective. So goals are important. They provide the focus, motivation, and energy that make teams successful.

While establishing goals may seem simple, one team I worked with took over three hours to agree on their goals. The problem was that this team had three developers, two testers, a requirements person, someone from the support group, and the team leader, and their interests and objectives were widely divergent. The goals discussion helped them to understand each others' objectives and to agree on what was important.

As leader, your actions are highly visible and your behavior is seen by your team as an example. Lee Iacocca once said, "The speed of the boss is the speed of the team."[1] You cannot expect your team to be any more committed or to work any harder or more carefully than you do. To get a full day's work from your people, you must put in a full day's work yourself. If you are not concerned about a one-day schedule slip, you cannot expect your people to work hard to make it up. If you don't seem to care about quality, usability, planning, or any of the other key aspects of the job, you can't expect your people to be concerned about these things either. Your energy, enthusiasm, and discipline set an example; when you take shortcuts, forget about the process, or ignore quality, so will your team. So remember to lead by what you do as well as by what you say.

The goals define what you and your team are supposed to do, but you are also responsible for how well that job is done. This is a matter of standards. A **standard** is a required level of performance or attainment, a comparator for quality, or a measure of acceptability. In engineering, there are many ways to measure and assess the work, but you are the only one who can monitor the team's performance and ensure that it meets the relevant standards.

There is an old saying in engineering: "If it doesn't have to work, we can build it pretty quickly." The essence of engineering is quality. Poor quality work is expensive, produces unsuccessful products, and is unsatisfying. Poor quality work wastes your time and your team's time, and it wastes your organization's money. Most developers intuitively understand the importance of quality and many even know how to do quality work. However, they often are not sufficiently skilled, motivated, and disciplined and don't have the leadership required to consistently produce quality results.

---

1. Lee Iacocca and William Novak. 1984. *Iacocca: An Autobiography*. New York: Bantam Books, 95.

One of the key standards for a development team leader is the ability to get quality work from his or her team. Motivate your people to do the job correctly and, if they don't do it properly the first time, get them to do it over until it is right. If you settle for sloppy, incomplete, or inaccurate work, a sloppy and lazy attitude will infect everything that the team does.

Even more important than the quality standard is the team's standard of cooperation and support. While this standard is rarely stated or explicit, it is the team members' cooperative and supportive behavior that makes the working environment rewarding, productive, and fun. As pointed out earlier, a top leadership priority must be providing a cohesive and cooperative working environment. Accomplishing this is almost entirely a matter of behavior: your behavior, your management's behavior, and every team member's behavior. So, setting and meeting behavioral standards for yourself, for your team members, and for your management must be your top priority.

## 8.3 LEARN TO AVOID THE SYMPTOMS OF POOR LEADERSHIP

To see why leadership is important, consider what its absence would mean. Have you ever worked in an organization that had an ineffective leader? You most likely have, and so have I.

My first brush with incompetent leadership was in one of my first engineering jobs. I was leading a team that was developing a military computer/communications system. This was a pretty advanced system, at least for the technology of the day, and I thought it had considerable commercial potential. I had convinced my immediate manager to launch a project to commercialize this military product and had also convinced the next higher layers of managers. Now I was in a meeting with the laboratory director.

After explaining this new product, I asked for his approval and support for a development effort. The laboratory director only asked me one question: "How long would it take for this product to become profitable?" I told him that it would probably be between 5 and 10 years before this product returned its initial investment and made a profit. He then said, "But I retire in four years." I thanked the director for his time, folded my papers, and walked out, and that very afternoon I started looking for another job. I knew that this kind of narrow, parochial management would never survive the rigors of the competitive marketplace that any commercial product would face. In fact, even though this was an old company that had been highly respected, it was soon acquired by a larger company and no longer exists.

What are the symptoms of poor leadership? As this story illustrates, the first and most obvious symptom is self-centered, parochial, or narrow-minded thinking by senior management. These managers are so concerned about their current issues, problems, and interests that they can't see beyond their own narrow personal horizons.

Another and very common symptom of poor leadership is what I call "bureaucratic momentum." This is the "don't-rock-the-boat" environment where next year's budgets are determined by adding a percentage to this year's budgets. Whatever is being done now is justified, and anything new or any proposed changes must fight for survival. While this approach is common in most large organizations, at least for much of their operations, it has the unfortunate consequence of building entrenched, bureaucratic, and inefficient groups.

One illustration of this phenomenon was in the British army. Shortly after World War II, staff writers were preparing a new manual for artillery crews, and they could not understand why there was a fifth person on each gun crew. The writers asked everyone in army headquarters. Finally, one senior officer suggested that they call the retired general who had written the original manual. The retired general knew immediately what the fifth person was supposed to do. "Why," he said, "he holds the horses."

The British army had not used horses for over 20 years, but the old manuals had never been updated and the gun crews continued to have a fifth person to hold the nonexistent horses. With a bureaucratic leadership style, no one tries to eliminate the obsolete jobs or to reexamine the organization's resource distribution in light of current priorities, technologies, and goals.

Another characteristic of poor leadership is management's inability to make effective decisions in a timely way. This problem usually results from a lack of vision. Management has no clearly defined concept for what the organization should be in the future, so there is no sound basis for setting priorities or allocating resources. One symptom of this problem is the common corporate obsession with growth: our goal is to grow at 15 percent a year, or we strive to grow as fast as the industry. However, size is not a vision. Do these companies offer anything unique, do they contribute to society, or do they develop powerful new products or services? Without a meaningful goal, there can be no leadership.

While there are many symptoms of poor leadership, my final example is the leadership style that is so obsessed with change that the organization is in perpetual turmoil. Managers in these organizations do not recognize that people work most effectively in a stable environment. Productivity is directly related to workplace stability and changes must be parceled out at a rate and in doses that do not saturate an organization's tolerance for disruption. By exceeding that capacity, executives can quickly destroy an otherwise capable organization.

As a team leader, you will not generally face the problems of organization-wide change. However, it is important to consider the common symptoms of poor leadership and to ensure that your leadership style does not create similar problems. Poor leadership has many symptoms, but it generally stems from a failure to see what is needed and to set a direction that takes advantage of the available resources and opportunities.

It is often difficult to be objective and to establish goals for what to do and how to do it, but the key is to realize that you do not need to do it all by yourself. The modern world is simply too complex and no one person is smart enough or has enough knowledge to figure out everything without assistance. While you likely must make many leadership decisions yourself, you should take advantage of the intelligence, ideas, and creative suggestions of your team.

There is ample evidence that the combined intelligence of a group produces better results than even the most skilled and talented individual.[2] So use your team. It needs leadership; it wants leadership; and it will gladly help you to provide that leadership.

## 8.4 LEADERSHIP MUST BE EARNED

Management uses resources to accomplish results; leadership motivates people to achieve objectives. Managing is impersonal and can be demeaning. It presumes that those being managed don't have ideas and feelings and must be told what to do and how to do it. Management is appropriate for handling inanimate objects or routine jobs. However, people like to be motivated to accomplish more challenging tasks, and they do not like being herded and directed as if they were so many cattle.

---

2. Watts S. Humphrey. 1997. *Managing Technical People: Innovation, Teamwork, and the Software Process.* Reading, MA: Addison-Wesley.

Most of us enjoy technical work, and we sought development careers because we like to do creative and challenging things. We also like to see the results of our labors, particularly when our products work the way we intended. But when someone treats us as if we were stupid or unthinking, we lose our energy and creative spark. As team leader, you will probably have to manage at least some routine work, but development engineering calls for leadership and for energetic and motivated teams. That is the only way to consistently produce truly superior results.

One principal distinction between leaders and managers is that managers direct people to obey their orders while leaders lead them. This crucial distinction is best illustrated by an example. One software manager, Ben, told me how he learned what leadership was all about. He was a marine lieutenant in Vietnam and, for the first time, he was leading his platoon into combat. As they approached the front lines, the captain told him, "Take that hill." "That hill" was where the enemy was dug in with a machine gun. There was no time for a discussion, so Ben told his troops, "Follow me," and he started running up the hill. He told me that all he could think of as he ran was not whether he would get shot or what would happen if he got to the top. The question that kept running through his head was, "Are they following?" It turned out that they were and they took the hill, but Ben told me that he learned right then that the two key ingredients of leadership are getting out front and trusting your troops to follow.

So leadership is intensely personal. It is not something that you can order and it is not something that you can measure, evaluate, and test. It is a property like loyalty or trust. It cannot be bought or inherited. It must be earned, and earned through long and often painful experience. It can, however, be lost in an instant. All you need to do is to stop behaving like a leader. Then your followers will stop following. They may continue to obey you, but you will soon sense that you no longer have their loyalty and trust. You can only tell if you are a leader by what happens: you are leading and they are following their leader.

What sets leaders apart from everyone else is that they have followers, and what attracts followers is a challenging and rewarding goal. It is impossible to be an effective leader without being committed to a cause that animates you and motivates your followers. Your energy and drive then come from your personal commitment to accomplish this objective.

This can't be just any goal—it must be something that you feel strongly about and will strive to accomplish. You must be sufficiently committed to this goal so that you can exhort your troops to achieve it, in spite of all obstacles. While development projects can have this character, that is not always the case. But, as we shall see, it is usually possible to excite creative people about the challenges and rewards of producing something entirely new and original.

## 8.5 STRIVE TO BE A TRANSFORMATIONAL LEADER

How do you feel about the job you have to do? Are you excited about it and dying to be part of creating this marvelous new product? If you view the job as just another chore, you have little chance of building the team's excitement to the feverish pitch required for great work. Excitement is contagious, but so are boredom and laziness. As a leader you not only set the team's pace, but you also establish the attitude. If you want this team to win, they must act like winners. And for them to act like winners, you must act like a winner and also treat them as winners. It all starts with you.

Think about your job and what you can do to make it an exciting project where people will want to work. If you wake up in the middle of the night with ideas on how to attack a major challenge, share your enthusiasm and excitement with the team. When your people have great ideas or accomplish a key task, cheer them on and help them celebrate. Involve the whole team and make this a rewarding and fun place to work.

Getting people excited about a goal, and convincing them to follow you to achieve it, is called **intrinsic motivation** or **transformational leadership**.[3] This is in contrast to the more mundane working situations called **extrinsic motivation** or **transactional leadership**. Transactional leadership is where you essentially make a deal with your people: "If you will do this job, I will reward you with a salary, a pay increase, or some other compensation." The distinction between these two kinds of leadership is in the motivation involved. With transformational leadership, your team is striving to achieve an objective. While the financial and other rewards are important, the real objective is the achievement, not just the reward. With transactional leadership, the true objective is the promised payment and the project is just a necessary step to obtaining it.

With transactional leadership comes all the problems of defining appropriate rewards, measuring achievements, and ensuring that people merit what they earn. This leads to the practical problems of measuring piece work, managing sales commissions, and so forth. In all of these cases, the workers' objectives and yours are diametrically opposed: they want to minimize the work required to get their payments, while you want to get the maximum work done for any given reward. Unfortunately, neither of you is totally focused on doing a creative and productive job.[4]

3. Watts S. Humphrey. 1997. *Managing Technical People: Innovation, Teamwork, and the Software Process.* Reading, MA: Addison-Wesley.

4. Robert D. Austin. 1996. *Measuring and Managing Performance in Organizations.* New York: Dorset House Publishing.

When people are not intrinsically motivated by their work, they generally find creative ways to do less work while earning more money. Since this attitude hardly makes for successful or creative projects, your objective must be transformational leadership.

## 8.6 LEADERS ARE MADE BY THEIR CIRCUMSTANCES

If you are in a leadership situation for the first time, you may wonder how you can meet all of the requirements. Many people view leaders as having a special charisma, vision, and energy that is quite out of the ordinary. But leaders aren't born, they are made; more often than not, they are made by their circumstances.

For example, one of the principal distinctions between superior troops and poorly led ones is in their leadership. In many armies, when a unit's officer is killed, that unit is disabled. But with superior military units, when the officer is killed, a sergeant steps forward to fill the leadership role. And if there is no sergeant, a corporal or private takes over. While these aren't born leaders, they know that the troops have to be led so they step in and do the job.

Harry Truman, for example, was a failed businessman who became an unremarkable congressman. Then Franklin Delano Roosevelt picked him to be his vice president. When FDR died, Truman became one of the most effective leaders of the free world. He had a job to do and he did it to the best of his ability. He created the Marshall Plan, launched the United Nations, and fought the Korean War. Then he had the guts to fire General Douglas MacArthur, a national icon, when the general wouldn't follow orders. In my mind, what set Truman apart was his basic humility and personal honesty. He never pretended to know something he didn't know, and he didn't hesitate to ask for advice. But when he had to make a decision, he did so, and he did it to the best of his ability without worrying about who agreed or how it would affect his reputation.

Like many seemingly ordinary people, when thrust into a challenging situation, Truman did a remarkable job. There is no reason that this approach can't work for you. If you are open and honest, get the best help you can find, and keep your eyes fixed on the goal, you too can be a great leader.

When you are a member of a team and are made the leader, it will usually take some time to realize that you are no longer just one of the boys (or girls). While you will almost certainly have the same nickname and eat the same lunch with the same crowd, you are no longer just any old team member—you are the leader.

While being a leader will not make you any smarter or give you any special insight or added knowledge, you now have a responsibility and you carry that responsibility into every situation. When the team is confused or doesn't know how to proceed, you can no longer hope that somebody else will step forward—you have to make sure the confusion is cleared up. While you do not have to solve every problem, you must make sure that the right steps are taken to find a solution. Once you become a leader, you are out front, in the lead, and in charge. And you are always in charge, even during coffee breaks, on vacation, or when you are asleep.

## 8.7 LEADING FROM BELOW

A lot has been written about the job of leading large corporations. It seems that every retired CEO wants to write a memoir that includes his or her personal "10 rules of effective leadership." While these rules are usually interesting and often useful, they don't address the most common leadership issue that I see in large organizations. This issue concerns the department or team leaders that are way down in the organization's hierarchy, and how these "subordinate leaders" behave. Most of these leaders rarely meet a senior executive; as a result, they don't have executive role models to emulate.

The essential problem of subordinate leadership is working in an organization that appears to be incompetent. In large organizations, the senior managers are often forced to make decisions about subjects that their subordinate managers know a great deal more about than they do. One of the best examples of this problem is a situation that developed shortly after I took over as IBM's Director of Programming. Our two largest locations were in Poughkeepsie, New York, and San Jose, California. Because the Poughkeepsie group had grown to nearly 1,000 developers and because it still needed many more people to handle its committed work, we had decided to move the data-management mission from Poughkeepsie to San Jose. The problem was that the interface between the Poughkeepsie operating system work and the San Jose data management products had not been defined.

We had told the two groups to agree on the interface definition and to come to me if they could not. Unfortunately, the interface definition had become a highly contentious issue with no clearly best answer and the two groups were unable to agree. One morning, the two laboratory managers with about thirty of their best technical people showed up in my office with two competing proposals. Although I knew less about this subject than anyone else in the room, I ended up designing the interface. I told the groups to either make my definition work or to agree on a better solution and to let me know what they agreed on. They never came back.

While in retrospect I can think of better ways to handle this issue, it is a good example of the kinds of decisions senior managers and executives have to make all of the time. Your job as a subordinate manager or team leader is either to make these decisions come out right or figure out how to change them so that they are right. Unfortunately, even when subordinate managers do this, they also often complain loudly to their teams about "those dummies upstairs." The messages this complaining attitude sends to the team are the following.

- I wasn't party to this decision and I can't be blamed if it doesn't come out right.
- I didn't agree with this decision and I am unable to get it changed.
- This place is badly run and does not have much of a future.
- When I get a better offer, I am out of here.

Even if this is how you feel, as a leader, you will damage yourself by saying it or even implying it. Do your job, motivate the team, and don't spend your time carping about what a terrible place this is to work, even if you feel that way. As a leader, you do have some limited power and you must decide where to apply it. While lots of the issues you see may be annoying, concentrate on those that really impact the job and don't complain about the others. Of course, when asked by your superiors, offer suggestions on how to fix the bureaucratic nonsense that you and your team deal with. Otherwise, concentrate on the important stuff and don't let these bureaucratic annoyances get you down.

## SOURCES

**8.1:** From *TSP^{SM}: Leading a Development Team*, Chapter 1

**8.2:** From *TSP^{SM}: Leading a Development Team*, Chapter 1

**8.3:** From *TSP^{SM}: Leading a Development Team*, Chapter 2

**8.4:** From *TSP^{SM}: Leading a Development Team*, Chapter 2

**8.5:** From *TSP^{SM}: Leading a Development Team*, Chapter 2

**8.6:** From *TSP^{SM}: Leading a Development Team*, Chapter 2

**8.7:** From *TSP^{SM}: Leading a Development·Team*, Chapter 2

# Epilogue

## Software Engineers Are the Pioneers of Knowledge Work

This excerpt is courtesy of the Computer History Museum, "Oral History of Watts Humphrey," 2009[1]

Peter Drucker, the famed writer, professor, and management consultant, wrote extensively about knowledge work and knowledge workers. He made a point that I think is enormously perceptive: You can't manage knowledge workers. They have to manage themselves.

What's astounding to me is, one, that's a terribly perceptive point, and two, no one has picked up on it anywhere. Everywhere you turn someone says, "Sure, that's true. They've got to manage themselves. Let's have them manage themselves. Great!" But the knowledge workers don't know how to do that. So it's a fundamental change in the whole management system to do that. And Peter Drucker clearly thought through that, but he wasn't in a position to go do it and make it happen.

That's the question that I have been struggling with for the TSP and the PSP. The question I had, and I think I mentioned

---

1. Interview conducted by Grady Booch. Available online at the Computer History Museum: http://www.computerhistory.org/collections/accession/102702107.

when I started with the CMM and then moved on to the PSP and TSP, was to look at how individual developers would really do software if they did it right. A big part of that was learning to be a personal manager, learning to make your own schedule, track your own progress, and manage the quality of your own work, to make commitments and to consistently meet them.

How could individuals do that? That's the framework on which the TSP and PSP are built, giving people the tools to do that. As you probably know, with most software folk, you tell them to do something and unless they really know how to do it, they'll probably put it off. At IBM, the software people had an enormous number of things to do, but there were only two they really had to do before they could ship a product. That was code and test. So they never got around to anything else. That's exactly true of the software community. You tell them, "What you really need to do is get your requirements nailed down and do inspections and do all this and that." And the question most of them have is, "Well, how do I do that?" They by and large don't know. They've never gone through that. They don't have a framework to do that. They don't have a process or guidance on how to do it. It's hard to find people who can. So they start off coding. I mean, they start off trying to put together a design. "Let's start building the product. We don't have time to wait."

That's the issue we run into in the software business. The people really are so busy, they're under such enormous pressure, that they just can't take the time to figure out how to do something. That's very obvious. I've got all kinds of data on how long it takes to develop a process, and the TSP process that I developed, with all the guidelines and the scripts and stuff like that, was several hundred hours of work. And I'd been developing processes for years. Software developers just don't have the time to do that. They'll use what they can get their hands on.

They're very pragmatic. They'll use my process if they know about it, and they're convinced it will work. And that's why with the PSP—which I developed, by the way—every time I wrote a program with it, I would sort of modify it and update it. When I write programs, I want to change the instruction set. When I work and use a process, I like to fix it and adjust it. I don't change it on that particular project, but I'll make notes and I'll go back and fix it.

I'm constantly evolving my process, but I find engineers don't do that. By and large, they use whatever process they've got. If it works, they're happy and they use it. So we learn from it when people use our processes, and we update them to make them more convenient. But the developers won't do it. They aren't willing to take the time. They don't have the time. "Just tell the developers to manage themselves." Managing themselves takes a lot of work. People have got to be able to find out what their requirements are. They've got to understand what management's goals are. They've got to put together an overall plan and strategy for how they're going to do it. They've got to negotiate their schedules and commitments with management, all of that stuff. Then they've got to do the work and they've got to track their progress; they've got to handle it.

There's an enormous number of things to do, and without guidance they can't do it. By the way, they also need room from management. Management has got to really take the time to meet with these people and say, "Here's what we want and why." That's what the launch process does, and it's extraordinarily effective. The whole idea of it is to actually give the developers and their teams the power to figure out what it takes to do the job. So when management assigns a project to a team, the team goes off and takes several days to put together a plan to do it, and they really crawl through it and they do a thorough job.

They've got historical data, either on their work or other teams' work. They'll go through and make a plan.

When they've finished, they know what it'll take to do the job and they have so much confidence in what they've done, and so much conviction, that when they present their story to management, management doesn't argue with them. I mean, basically, these people know. They've got the conviction. The management is universally impressed with the teams when they come back. They've got credibility, so they negotiate with management. The teams always end up winning, and they've done that time and again.

I remember one case—this was a good many years ago now. It was a team at the Ford Motor Company. It was a small team. This team had started a project; I think there were five engineers on it. Management had gone through with them and given them the goals where you had to get this done in a year. Management's reason to have it in a year was that they had a market window and they had cost limitations. Well, it turned out to be an enormously ambitious project, and the team basically went through it and came back and presented the story to management and said, "Look, with this team, this will take five years. If you want to put 20 some people on it, we can probably bring it in a lot closer, but no way we can get to a year, and here's what we've got to do."

They went through the story and management said, "Let's think about that." And then they canceled the project. Well, that's an enormous success. What teams typically do is, management tells them they've got to do it in a year. "Okay, chief." Then the team will say: "We'll try." They'll break their hump for about eight or nine months and management says, "Where are you?" They'll come back, "Oh, it'll be another six or eight months." And so the delay will keep going and they'll lengthen the schedule. After about two and a half years, they will have gotten where they're working under enormous pressure. They don't do the work right. There are all kinds of problems. Then they kill the project, and they waste a lot of money, they waste a lot of the engineers' time. Nobody wants to do that.

So having reality on the table right away, by and large, with very few exceptions, that works. But we do run into a few cases. I remember one case in one company, which I won't name. The senior vice president had basically given a directive: "You'll get this project out by this date." The lab manager and the team were scared to death, because this VP was unwilling to come to the lab and talk to the team. He was unwilling to listen to what they were doing. It was all done remotely. The last time somebody had gone back to him and told him they couldn't do it, they fired him.

So they finally concluded there was no way they were going to do this. This guy was dealing through a pipe. He didn't have the guts or self-confidence to deal with his people directly and he was totally unreasonable. And so they did not use the TSP, and about a year and a half later, the lab director was fired, and so was the VP. I mean, this sort of thing goes on all the time. It's crazy. And so you do get a few nuts like that in the management chain but not too many. Most of them are smart enough to know that when the team really says they can't do it on this schedule, that's probably true. The problem is that few teams know enough to say they can't do it on management's schedule. If they did, then we wouldn't have so many disasters.

So the point I'm making here is that the teams discover that when they have data and they have facts, they can talk to anybody. I mean, we've had cases where brand new engineers, with a year or two of experience, going through this stuff, will explain something to a senior vice president, and the senior VP buys it, because the engineers have the data and they understand what they're talking about, and they've got conviction. What these engineers discover is, they've got enormous power that they never had before, and they're able to actually negotiate schedules that make sense. Their work is a hell of a lot more fun. They work at a reasonable schedule, and it works. It works extraordinarily well.

Let me talk about one case in India, one of the Microsoft projects. They'd done a great job and I was there reviewing their results. They had just come off a previous project, which was an absolute disaster. They worked 70-hour weeks; they were late. The project had all kinds of problems in test. It was a mess. And so they decided to learn the PSP and do the TSP on the next project. So this was the first TSP project that they'd done, the very first one.

In the launch, the team had gone through and said, "We've got a team goal of working 40-hour weeks. We're also obviously going to meet the schedule and all that sort of stuff." But they had a team goal of working 40-hour weeks. I was reviewing the results of the project. They said, "We didn't quite make our goal. We worked 45-hour weeks on average, but it was a hell of an improvement over 70." They were home for dinner. It was an experience they enjoyed. It was great. They delivered on schedule to test. The product sailed through test without any particular problems at all, and the team was just terribly excited about it.

So we see engineers, software folk, all of a sudden becoming heroes instead of bums. And these people deserve to be heroes. They're bright; they're capable. They do marvelous work, but at the moment, they are suffering under this cloud, because they really don't have the skills to manage themselves.

The reason this is an important issue is because knowledge work—this is back to Peter Drucker—knowledge work, the first real large-scale knowledge work, was in software. Years and years ago, when I started, I'd done all the hardware stuff. I could manage 30, 40, 50 people doing hardware work. I could walk around. I knew where things were. I didn't have any problems. But even with a team of 10 software people, unless I was really willing to take the time and really sit down and go through with each one what was going on, there's no way I could know what they were doing.

As Fred Brooks once said, they're 90 percent through coding most of the time. The software people have no idea where they are typically today. So you go ask them where you are, and they'll go, "Oh yeah, I'm on schedule. I'll be in to test shortly." They literally don't know when they'll be done. So all of that, the lack of skills and all of that, we end up with people who have no credibility with their management. They end up getting pushed into commitments they can't meet; they're failures. They'll work god-awful hours and we see that throughout the field. It is not the kind of industry that is going to be healthy and growing over time, the way it's being run today.

# Appendix
# PSP, TSP, and CMMI

The essays in this book make frequent reference to three process methodologies for which Watts Humphrey led design efforts as a senior fellow at the Software Engineering Institute (SEI) of Carnegie Mellon University: the Capability Maturity Model (CMM), the Personal Software Process (PSP), and the Team Software Process (TSP). For extensive information on these topics, see the Watts Humphrey books listed in the bibliography and visit the SEI website at www.sei.cmu.edu. The following are brief descriptions of these three methodologies.

## THE PERSONAL SOFTWARE PROCESS (PSP)[1]

The Personal Software Process (PSP) is based on the following planning and quality principles:

- Every engineer is different; to be most effective, engineers must plan their work, and they must base their plans on their own personal data.

- To consistently improve their performance, engineers must personally use well-defined and measured processes.

---

1. Source: Watts S. Humphrey. 2000. *The Personal Software Process (PSP)*. CMU/SEI-2000-TR-022. Pittsburgh, PA: Software Engineering Institute. Available online at http://www.sei.cmu.edu/reports/00tr022.pdf.

- To produce quality products, engineers must feel personally responsible for the quality of their products. Superior products are not produced by mistake; engineers must strive to do quality work.

- It costs less to find and fix defects earlier in a process than later.

- It is more efficient to prevent defects than to find and fix them.

- The right way is always the fastest and cheapest way to do a job.

To do a software engineering job in the right way, engineers must plan their work before committing to or starting on a job, and they must use a defined process to plan the work. To understand their personal performance, they must measure the time that they spend on each job step, the defects that they inject and remove, and the sizes of the products they produce. To consistently produce quality products, engineers must plan, measure, and track product quality, and they must focus on quality from the beginning of a job. Finally, they must analyze the results of each job and use these findings to improve their personal processes.

Starting with a requirements statement, the first step in the PSP process is planning. There is a planning script that guides this work and a plan summary for recording the planning data. While the engineers are following the script to do the work, they record their time and defect data on the time and defect logs. At the end of the job, during the postmortem phase, they summarize the time and defect data from the logs, measure the program size, and enter these data in the plan summary form. When done, they deliver the finished product along with the completed plan summary form.

## THE TEAM SOFTWARE PROCESS (TSP)[2]

To do disciplined work, engineers need what W. Edwards Deming calls "operational processes."[3] These are processes that define precisely how the work is to be done. While most poorly defined software processes are large and comprehensive text descriptions that are filed in process definition books, an operational process is more like a script. It is designed to be used by the team members when they do the work.

The Team Software Process (TSP) provides a defined operational process to guide engineers and managers through the team-building steps. This process specifies the steps needed to establish an effective teamworking environment. Without specific guidance, engineers must work out the details of team-building and teamworking for themselves. Since defining these details involves considerable skill and effort, and since few engineers have the experience or time to work out all of the necessary details, engineering teams generally follow ad hoc team-building and teamwork processes. This wastes time, and it often produces poorly functioning teams.

With a defined process and a plan that follows that process, engineers can be highly efficient. If they don't have such a process, they must stop at each step to figure out what to do next and how to do it. Most engineering processes are quite complex and involve many steps. Without specific guidance, engineers are likely to skip steps, to do steps in an unproductive order, or to waste time figuring out what to do next. The TSP provides the operational processes needed to form engineering teams, to

---

2. Source: Watts S. Humphrey. 2000. *The Team Software Process (TSP)*. CMU/ SEI-2000-TR-023. Pittsburgh, PA: Software Engineering Institute. Available online at http://www.sei.cmu.edu/reports/00tr023.pdf.

3. W. Edwards Deming. 1982. *Out of the Crisis*. Cambridge, MA: MIT Center for Advanced Engineering Study.

establish an effective team environment, and to guide teams in doing the work.

Before team members can participate on a TSP team, they must know how to do disciplined work. Training in the Personal Software Process (PSP) is required to provide engineers with the knowledge and skills to use the TSP.

While there are many ways to build teams, they all require that the individuals work together to accomplish some demanding task. In the TSP, this demanding team-building task is a two- to four-day planning process that is called the team launch. In a launch, all the team members develop the strategy, process, and plan for doing their project. After completing the launch, the team follows its own defined process to do the job. Because the TSP process follows an iterative and evolving development strategy, periodic relaunches are necessary so that each phase or cycle can be planned based on the knowledge gained in the previous cycle. The relaunch is also required to update the engineers' detailed plans, which are usually accurate for only a few months.

## CMM AND CMMI

Capability Maturity Model Integration (CMMI) is a process improvement maturity model for the development of products and services. It consists of best practices that address development and maintenance activities that cover the product lifecycle from conception through delivery and maintenance.

The Capability Maturity Model (CMM) for Software, described in 1991 in an SEI technical report,[4] was a process improvement approach that provided organizations with the essential elements

---

4. Software Engineering Institute. 1991. *Capability Maturity Model for Software.* CMU/SEI-1991-TR-024. Pittsburgh, PA: Software Engineering Institute.

of effective processes to ultimately improve their performance. The CMM for Software was later adapted for other disciplines, such as systems engineering and integrated product development. This integration, however, created challenges: Organizations that wished to apply more than one model found that overlaps and conflicts in content and differences in architecture and guidance increased the cost and difficulty of organization-wide improvement. To address these conflicts, the Department of Defense initiated the Capability Maturity Model Integration (CMMI) project in 1997 to establish a framework to accommodate current and future models and to bring the CMM approach in line with international industry standards. Since then, models from this methodology have used the label CMMI, rather than CMM.

# Bibliography

Grady Booch, interviewer. 2009. "Humphrey (Watts) Oral History." Computer History Museum. Available online at http://www.computerhistory.org/collections/accession/102702107.

Watts S. Humphrey. 1995. *A Discipline for Software Engineering*. Reading, MA: Addison-Wesley.

Watts S. Humphrey. 1997. *Introduction to the Personal Software Process$^{SM}$*. Reading, MA: Addison-Wesley.

Watts S. Humphrey. 1997. *Managing Technical People: Innovation, Teamwork, and the Software Process*. Reading, MA: Addison-Wesley.

Watts S. Humphrey. 2000. *Introduction to the Team Software Process$^{SM}$*. Boston, MA: Addison-Wesley.

Watts S. Humphrey. 2000. The Personal Software Process (PSP). CMU/SEI-2000-TR-022. Pittsburgh, PA: Software Engineering Institute. Available online at http://www.sei.cmu.edu/reports/00tr022.pdf.

Watts S. Humphrey. 2000. The Team Software Process (TSP). CMU/SEI-2000-TR-023. Pittsburgh, PA: Software Engineering Institute. Available online at http://www.sei.cmu.edu/reports/00tr023.pdf.

Watts S. Humphrey. 2002. *Winning with Software: An Executive Strategy*. Boston, MA: Addison-Wesley.

Watts S. Humphrey. 2005. *PSP$^{SM}$: A Self-Improvement Process for Software Engineers*. Boston, MA: Addison-Wesley.

Watts S. Humphrey. 2006. *TSP^{SM}: Coaching Development Teams*. Boston, MA: Addison-Wesley.

Watts S. Humphrey. 2006. *TSP^{SM}: Leading a Development Team*. Boston, MA: Addison-Wesley.

Watts S. Humphrey. 2008. "The Software Quality Challenge." *CrossTalk: The Journal of Defense Software Engineering*, June 2008. Available online at http://www.stsc.hill.af.mil/crosstalk/2008/06/0806Humphrey.html.

Watts S. Humphrey. 2009. *The Watts New Collection: Columns by the SEI's Watts Humphrey.* CMU/SEI-2009-SR-024. Pittsburgh, PA: Software Engineering Institute. Available online at http://www.sei.cmu.edu/library/abstracts/reports/09sr024.cfm.

# Index

# FREE Online Edition

Your purchase of **Reflections on Management** includes access to a free online edition for 45 days through the Safari Books Online subscription service. Nearly every Addison-Wesley Professional book is available online through Safari Books Online, along with more than 5,000 other technical books and videos from publishers such as Cisco Press, Exam Cram, IBM Press, O'Reilly, Prentice Hall, Que, and Sams.

**SAFARI BOOKS ONLINE** allows you to search for a specific answer, cut and paste code, download chapters, and stay current with emerging technologies.

## Activate your FREE Online Edition at www.informit.com/safarifree

> **STEP 1:** Enter the coupon code: OFVUNCB.

> **STEP 2:** New Safari users, complete the brief registration form. Safari subscribers, just log in.

If you have difficulty registering on Safari or accessing the online edition, please e-mail customer-service@safaribooksonline.com